American Food & California Wine

BARBARA KAFKA

ILLUSTRATED BY DALE GLASSER

HARPER & ROW, PUBLISHERS, New York

Cambridge, Philadelphia, San Francisco, London

Mexico City, São Paulo, Sydney

IRENA CHALMERS COOKBOOKS, INC., New York

To My Family

ACKNOWLEDGMENTS

When one works as I do, as a member of a team, it is sometimes hard to know where I stop and where the other parts of the team begin. I would like to thank the team and assure them that I remember. I lift a glass of the very best to Lois Bloom, Susan Frank, Jane Helsel, Paula Wolfert, Judy Thompson, Amalia Pena and Carl Jerome.

I thank those from whom I have learned: the friends whose dinners delight, the chefs, the writers, past and present, and the people I have worked for. The best part is that there is always more to learn, more to eat and more to drink.

FIRST HARPER & ROW EDITION

Library of Congress Cataloging in Publication Data

Kafka, Barbara.
  American food & California wine.

  (Great American cooking schools series)
  Bibliography: p.
  1. Cookery, American. 2. Wine and wine making—California. I. Title.
II. Title: American food and California wine. III. Series.
TX715.K126 1982   641.5   82-47863
ISBN 0-06-015066-1

82 83 84 85 86 10 9 8 7 6 5 4 3 2 1

Contents

Foreword BY JAMES BEARD

Barbara Kafka never does anything commonplace.

I've known her since the days when she was editing *The Cooks' Catalogue.* I was a consultant on that book, and I well remember making the acquaintance of a slim, intense young woman with a restless, creative mind. Since then I've dined with her, taught with her and argued with her; and I've never failed to come away stimulated from any encounter with her. She has the rare gift of being able to take in a broad, often confusing, mass of information, and to make it clear and exciting to other people.

Now she's done this in an area that is especially dear to my heart, American food and wine. More and more, I think, the best culinary minds have become convinced that American food is on a par with any in the world. We have a glorious abundance of natural products. We have a real tradition—and heaven knows we should, after all these years. And we have young people with lots of creativity and imagination. When American food is good, it's very very good, and nothing but snobbery has prevented people from recognizing that fact.

But Mrs. Kafka is the last person to be influenced by such nonsense. With all of her appreciation of the finest in food and wine, she has, at the same time, a sense of the virtue of simple things (which are, after all, often the very best). She has made a specialty of learning about our native wines, becoming an expert in the classification and enjoyment of wines produced in California, Oregon, New York and Washington.

She knows that there are a great many wines, from America and elsewhere, which are simple of origin and make no pretension of being among the great vintages, but which can still be enjoyed and appreciated, especially when they are married to the right food.

That's what this book of hers is all about. On the one hand, there are the recipes: native, gratifying, yet none of them elaborate or taxing. It has been my privilege to taste quite a few of these recipes, both at Mrs. Kafka's home and while we were touring and teaching together. My impression is that they reflect the personality of their developer, which is the mark of truly creative work in any area.

Along with the recipes, Mrs. Kafka has given us a guide to understanding wine. She knows that most people can't afford the major vintages, but she wants them to be able to get the most from any wine they drink. It may be a jug wine. It may be a little-known bottle from a fairly unknown vineyard. But she believes—as I do, too—that it deserves to be treated with proper attention and judged by honest standards. She thinks the more you taste, the more you know, and the more you know, the more you will enjoy.

So: American foods and American wines: two great enthusiasms of mine and of Barbara Kafka's. I think all is well for the future of American cooking as long as we have young people with her talent and enthusiasm to keep up its traditions and to move it even farther ahead.

American Food

The development of a truly American culinary style is a subject of great excitement to both the eater and the cook in me. This is not a regional cuisine, nor a slavish imitation of the French or Chinese. We Americans have gone beyond that. We take our good local ingredients, combine them with the seasonings of the entire world, use the techniques we learned as we apprenticed ourselves to the teachers and writers who refined our savage tastes for the past 150 years, and thus create our own food.

We are no longer afraid to try out our own combinations. We cook to fit our lives, sometimes producing marvelous meals between the time we get home from work and the arrival of our guests. Health-conscious and desk-bound, we eat more lightly than our ancestors did. Thanks to central heating and air conditioning, our menus vary less from winter to summer than they used to, except as we respond to the availability of fruit and vegetables or the first soft-shell crabs.

We have a bountiful, diverse land. In previous times, before we built up and polluted much of our land and water, we were net exporters of caviar and fine wines. Today we are again beginning to cultivate these luxuries. As our tastes develop and new groups of immigrants bring a preference for their own necessities and delicacies, our land begins to yield Haitian, Indian and Thai delights as well.

Perhaps the new interest in wine is the best indicator of change in our eating tastes and habits. If Waverley Root, writing in the heyday of our veneration for French foods and wines, is correct, there is a necessary connection among the wines a country produces, the food it grows and cooks and eats, and the character of the minds and souls that this conjunction creates. The grapes of Germany, Italy, France, Spain and every other wine-growing nation jostle each other for a bit of our prolific soil, our enriching sun. Let our cooking be as various. Let us hope that our minds are as at home in the cultures of the world as are our wines.

California Wines

Wine is one of the world's great pleasures. Any place where people have lived and the climate has barely tolerated the grape, wine has been made. Cultures can be defined by whether they are viniferous or not. Certainly, in recent years America has become a wine-drinking nation.

Although the promise of Vinland was seen by Norse explorers in the 11th century and by the all-wise Thomas Jefferson in the 18th, it was not until the end of the 19th century that California's promise as a producer of fine wines for the nation began to be fulfilled. In 1919, Prohibition and a variety of natural and fiscal dramas put an abrupt end to this beginning.

Prohibition ended in 1933, but the Depression and the onset of war precluded much redevelopment of the vineyards. After the war, there were more pressing concerns than wine, as people took up their interrupted lives. Much of what had been vineyard became housing development. After a while, things settled down and wine began once more to come into its own. The 1950s belonged to the pioneers, the 1960s to the beginning of the current redevelopment. By the 1970s, we were beyond redevelopment and winemaking had become a full-blown new industry.

Nothing can be produced for long without a market. As new wines came into being and became available, the public responded by buying and drinking and becoming more adventurous. Wines went from sweetish to dry and from rosé to white. Now, the full diversity of what is available is being sought out and bought.

While this rapid and complex evolution has been all to the good in terms of quality and variety, it has created problems for the buyer and enjoyer of wine. There has been no long history during which names and techniques have gradually been developed and standardized. At the best of times, the subject of wine is complex. In these days, it is particularly hard to know what to do when selecting California wines to drink, because they are constantly changing.

This uncertainty is emphasized by our changing style of eating. In other places in the world, the same soil that has nourished the food of the area also produces the wine, and the two have gradually come to go together. Our foods are not historic—or only slightly so. They do not come from the same soil and suit the same climate as the wines we drink. We have to find new combinations to please ourselves.

Finding the Right Wine

How do we go about discovering these wines and finding out which wines please us with which foods? I hope this book will help. There has to be some balance between familiarity and experimentation. A good wine dealer—like a good butcher—is invaluable. With the dealer's guidance and by tasting critically, we can discover what we like—although this may change as we drink more wines.

Some people feel that a nation's wines are to be judged by the quality of those chosen for everyday drinking. If that is so, we are in very good shape. Both white and red what used to be called jug, and now are called table, wines are better in this country than they are anywhere in the world, especially at such moderate prices. An everyday wine is one whose character is general enough to permit it to be drunk with a wide variety of foods. Yet it must not be so vapid that we become quickly bored with it.

A good wine dealer will be willing to recommend a variety of wines at prices you think suitable. Buy a few and drink them with dinner on successive nights. If you find a red and a white that you like, buy a few bottles of each; drink them for a while with your meals and see how they stand the test of time. If they still seem good to you, you now have a wine-buying base. With time, you may not want to drink these wines except on rare occasions.

Most of the wines at the lower end of the price scale are blended and pasteurized or filtered. They tend to be made by large companies who view their wines primarily as merchandise. Understandably, these wines are less distinctive than wines made from a dominant grape and produced by a winemaker with a personal point of view. They do serve a purpose, however, in being relatively inexpensive and easy to consume.

The problems and the more acute pleasures come with the next step: getting from table wines to somewhat more distinctive wines. Even describing the wines is apt to be confusing, because of the special development of California wines; but I will try.

The Making of Wine

Wines are the product of many variables: grapes, men, soil and climate. It is hard to tell which of these is the most important. Men, of course, decide where the grapes are to be planted, how they are to be pruned, when and how they are to be picked, crushed and fermented—and they have a thousand more decisions to make about temperatures, yeasts, blending, aging, wood and bottling. Yet the nature of each variety of grape persists beyond man and land. Conversely, there are certain parcels of land—for instance, La Tâche in Burgundy—whose soil asserts itself in the wine: good years and bad, marvelous vinification and less good. While general climate is characteristic to a given area, specific elements of temperature and rainfall vary from year to year—that is, among vintages.

California has yet to sort itself out. There are no great historic associations of a given grape with a given piece of land. Perhaps we have been too fortunate. Almost everything grows everywhere in California; now it remains to be seen where it grows best. In the meantime, as consumers, we must taste wines and learn what grapes we like and which winemakers we trust to make a wine that suits our palates.

I am not going to discuss individual winemakers here, as they, like their wines, are in a constant state of ferment and change. What I can do is to identify the growing areas and the grapes so that we can make intelligent wine choices. I also hope to formulate some questions to ask about winemaking that will enable us to hazard a good guess as to whether or not we will like a particular wine.

Basic Wine Categories

Wines fall into two basic categories: table wines and fortified wines. Table wines normally contain from 10 to 14 percent alcohol, which is the product of naturally occurring yeast fermentation of the fruit sugar in the grapes. Under rare conditions some white Rieslings will have as little as 6 or 7 percent alcohol; some extraordinary Zinfandels have been made with as much as 16 percent alcohol. Normally, alcohol kills the yeasts at 14 to 15 percent.

Fortified wines are stabilized (meaning they won't turn to vinegar) and made much more alcoholic by the addition of distilled alcohol. While fortified wines—in the style of sherry, port and Madeira—are also made in California, they are not the subject of this book. I am discussing table wines because, as their name implies, they go with food, and because they are what I enjoy most.

Some California wines are pasteurized to keep them from changing. These are primarily mass-produced wines that are not intended to age. Their one advantage is that they will not deteriorate after they are opened. This is particularly useful to bars. However, most of the table wines that interest me are not stabilized; they continue to develop in the bottle.

Colors

Table wines exist in four broad categories: red, made from dark-skinned grapes and generally vinified dry; white, made from light-skinned grapes and either dry or sweet; rosé, made from dark-skinned grapes and either dry or slightly sweet; and sparkling wine, made from dark- or light-skinned grapes or a combination, and either dry or sweet. The last may be any of the three colors.

Red wines may actually vary in color from almost purple through burgundy and garnet with hints of brown and rust to light, clear reds just a step away from rosé. The color depends on the grapes that are used in the wine, its age, the kind of wood in which it has been aged, and, in unfortunate instances, oxidation.

White wine is, of course, not white. It may vary from a greenish tint through straw yellow all the way to gold. Some sweet white wines have slightly orange lights, and when old, a hint of ocher.

Rosé wines are hardly ever a true pink. They vary, as the red wines do, with the grape. They also vary in intensity of color depending on the amount of time the fermenting wine is left on the skins. Some of these wines have barely turned from the white toward the pink. These pale shades are described as having the color of onion skins or, more fancifully, that of partridges' eyes. I couldn't swear to the last myself, having never looked a partridge in the eye.

The rosé wine question is further complicated in California as a few winemakers—wishing to escape the negative associations of some rosé wine as a relatively inexpensive, undistinguished brew—give their rosés such names as Blanc de Pinot Noir, meaning white wine made from red Pinot grapes.

Sparkling wine, as I've said, can be almost any color. Red sparkling wine is to be avoided; it is almost always terrible. White sparkling wines can be made from either red or white grapes. In California, when such wines are made from red grapes, they generally pick up some color from the skins even before the crushing of the grapes is finished. Therefore, when you see the name of a red grape on the label, the chances are that the wine will be some variant of rosé and can be very good indeed.

Tastes

In addition to its color, wine gets almost all of its taste elements from the grapes. What it does not get from the grapes is the taste of wood, which comes from the barrels in which the wine ages, and the smell of the yeasts used in fermenting.

We tend to classify wines as basically dry or sweet. Dry simply means that there is no sugar left after the yeasts have fermented the grape juice and its sugar into wine. If there is any remaining sugar, it is called residual. Dryness is not necessarily an indication of quality. Some of the world's greatest wines, from Château d'Yquem in France, Tokay in Hungary, Riesling in Germany to Selected Late Harvest wines in California, are prized for their intentional sweetness. California sweet wines got a bad name through certain proprietors who made sweet jug wines from grapes that are not meant to yield sweet wines. The proprietors thought Americans would like only sweetish wines, as was largely true in the early days of the California wine industry.

As a guideline, it should be noted that wine with more than 6 percent residual sugar is very sweet and that we normally think of a wine with 2 percent residual sugar as sweet. The jug winemakers were producing red wines with as much as 2 percent residual sugar as late as the early 1970s. Today, even the mass-marketed wines have only half of 1 percent residual sugar.

Fruitiness

Even if a wine is completely dry, there are elements of its taste that may be confused with sweetness. A lack of acid is one such generally negative element. Another, which can be positive or negative, is the taste and smell of fruit. Wine is not meant to be simple grape juice, but a certain amount of fruitiness can be very pleasant in many wines. It is an almost invariable component of young wines. Red wines made from the Gamay grape and many white wines made from Riesling grapes are known for their fruitiness. But when a big red wine that is meant to age is described as "grapey," it is not a compliment.

Acids

Many of us think that to call a wine acid is to insult it. Indeed, if acidity is the overwhelming impression given by a wine, the wine is not pleasant. However, wine does need acid. Without it, a wine tastes flabby and uninteresting, without any sense of youthfulness.

There are many kinds of acids in grapes. Some are particularly present in green, unripe grapes. If the wine is made from grapes at this unripe stage, it will taste sour, like a mouth-puckering apple. Other desirable acids develop as the grapes mature. Some acids begin to evaporate as the grapes get riper. Picking the grapes at the proper stage—when they have good acid but not too much or too little—makes for good wine. Sometimes in California, where there is a great deal of sun, the grapes have lost too much acidity by the time they have fully matured, and the resulting wine is dull.

There is one very special acid in grapes and wine which tastes quite different from the others. This is tannic acid—very evident in tea. Generally, when this wine acid is being talked about, it is called tannin. Tannin is the backbone of wine taste. Without enough tannin, wine tastes spineless; with too much, it tastes harsh and unbending. Tannin comes primarily from the skin and pits of the grape. Therefore, red wine is generally more tannic than white. Unpleasant tannin has a bitterness, which occurs if the grapes have been crushed too brutally and the pits have been broken. Good tannin mellows with age, and that is why young white wines—low in tannin—are often more pleasant to drink than young reds.

Tannin and other acids give red wines the strength to hold up under the desirable aging process. Because tannin modifies with age and too much unmodified tannin is unpleasant, it is often very hard for anyone but an expert to judge a young wine that is destined for aging. This doesn't mean that you or I are not entitled to say that a young tannic wine is unpleasant. What it does mean is that we won't be able to judge what it will taste like when it is fully mature. Even the experts are only making educated guesses and can prove to be wrong.

Smell

Smell is as important to our sense of taste as what happens in our mouths. Wines have been described by analogy with many other scents—everything from roses and violets to apples and spices. Each grape variety seems to have its own particular scent, or "nose." This perfume also develops and changes with age.

Texture

There are various textural elements in wine that are perceived as part of the taste. Glycerine is a by-product of fermentation and increases with alcohol. It gives a wine a certain weight on the tongue, often described as "body." Glycerine also has a sweetish taste which can be confused with sugar.

Yeasts and Molds

There are some flavors in wine that are not intrinsic to the grape. The kind of yeast that is used to ferment the juice is one such element.

While there are naturally occurring yeasts on the skins of grapes and in the air, California winemakers prefer not to depend on these because they have no control over them; instead they introduce cultured yeasts into the wine.

As the wine ferments, the smells and tastes of the yeasts should bubble off into the air along with the escaping gases. Except in sparkling wines, where the smell and taste of yeast is characteristic, yeast should not be perceptible in the finished wine. Nor should the wine taste prickly on the tip of the tongue—another indication that all the work of the fermentation has not been completed.

One does not want any "dirty" tastes in the wine, such as are produced by yeasts and molds. There is one great exception to this rule—a mold called *Botrytis cinerea*, noble rot, which forms on ripe white grapes under certain conditions of moisture. This mold sucks moisture out of the grape, increasing its relative sugar content and intensifying its taste. Wine made from such grapes is rare and highly prized. It also has a characteristic smell of the *Botrytis*. Recently, to the delight of all, this mold has occurred in a number of harvests in small areas of grapes in California. It has produced some wonderful, albeit expensive, wines. One of the reasons for the high price of these wines is that the sucking out of the liquid leaves less juice per grape with which to make wine.

Barrels

The taste of wine is also influenced by the kind of barrel in which the wine is put to age. In California today, wines are generally put to ferment in stainless steel tanks that impart no taste to the fermenting wines; often, these are then put to age in wood. Increasingly, this is some kind of oak.

Wine Names and Varieties

Despite all the elements described above, wine's taste is primarily influenced by the specific variety of grape from which it is made.

Generic Wines

Most winemakers in California have European backgrounds or palates at least slightly influenced by European wines. It has also been found that the best California wines come from European grape varieties. It was perhaps natural, then, that at first the wines of California were given the names of wines from specific European wine-growing districts. In this way, we got California Chablis, Chianti and Burgundy. Wines so named are called generic. This is confusing, because these are the names of places as well as wines, and the wines with these names taste nothing like the originals. Even when the California wines are made from the same kind of grape as the European wines, the differences in soil and climate produce very different results.

Varietals

By and large this pattern is changing; most California wines today either are named after their dominant grape (varietals) or are given a proprietary name, which may be the name of the producer or a name made up specifically for that wine. The sole holdouts among the quality wines are the sparkling wines called Champagne. Champagne is also the name of a place, and so in this book I call these wines simply sparkling wines or "bubbly."

By California law, for a wine to be named after a grape it must be made from at least 51 percent of that grape. In fact, many of these wines are 100-percent varietal. There is a move afoot to raise the legal percentage to 75. While this seems logical, it does present some prob-lems. Certain varieties of grape, such as Cabernet Sauvignon and Merlot, have affinities for each other. Short of returning to the old, discredited nomenclature—for instance, Bordeaux—there would be no easy way to describe such a wine made under the new ruling if it were made with, say, 60 percent Cabernet and 40 percent Merlot.

Even when the grape variety is correctly named on the label, there can be confusion about what it means. If it is incorrectly named, this is usually intentionally done to mislead the public.

Varietal Names

The varietal names described below are the grape names you are most likely to see on bottles. There are also hybrid and less prestigious grapes, such as Thompson Seedless, that are grown along with the varieties mentioned here—particularly in the huge, hot San Joaquin Valley. These grapes-whose-names-are-never-mentioned, along with those grapes-whose-names-are-seldom-mentioned, are the basis of the so-called brand-name wine business. Part of the reason for this is historical. When Prohibition came along, table grapes—primarily Thompson Seedless—replaced the wine grapes that could not be sold. After Prohibition, these grapes, as well as others that are plentiful and richly yielding in juice, but are undistinguished varieties, were found to be perfect for the inexpensive fortified and brand-name wines, especially the sickly sweet ones that were popular at the time. During the difficult days of the Depression, wineries could survive and grow only by making plenty of inexpensive wine. Now even these grapes are vinified more dryly to become today's brand-name jug wines and the few remaining generic wines. Today varietal grapes are beginning to make their appearance

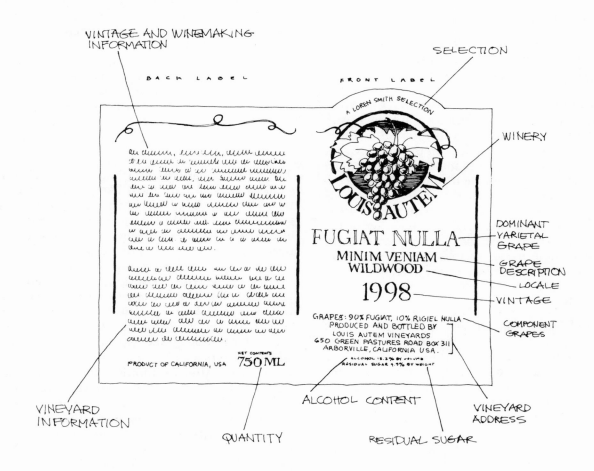

VINTAGE AND WINEMAKING
INFORMATION

SELECTION

BACK LABEL

FRONT LABEL

A LOREN SMITH SELECTION

WINERY

LOUIS AUTEM

FUGIAT NULLA
MINIM VENIAM
WILDWOOD
1998

DOMINANT
VARIETAL
GRAPE

GRAPE
DESCRIPTION

LOCALE

VINTAGE

GRAPES: 90% FUGIAT, 10% RIGIEL NULLA
PRODUCED AND BOTTLED BY
LOUIS AUTEM VINEYARDS
650 GREEN PASTURES ROAD BOX 311
ARBORVILLE, CALIFORNIA USA.

COMPONENT
GRAPES

ALCOHOL 15.2% BY VOLUME
RESIDUAL SUGAR 9.9% BY WEIGHT

NET CONTENTS
PRODUCT OF CALIFORNIA, USA   750 ML

VINEYARD
INFORMATION

QUANTITY

ALCOHOL CONTENT

RESIDUAL SUGAR

VINEYARD
ADDRESS

HOW TO READ A WINE LABEL

even in the San Joaquin Valley, as the public demand for better wines increases and as growers learn new ways of training their vines and spraying them so that the more delicate varieties can survive the heat.

Of the more popular varietals, those that are likely to be named on a label are of European origin except for Emerald Riesling, which is a California-developed variety. It is therefore probably inevitable that even when we do not call the wines these grapes produce by European names, we tend to compare the wines themselves with their European equivalents. I do it myself, and it will take a long time for me to change. I manage best to avoid the comparison with wines that have been splendidly successful on their own in California.

In a general guide such as this, I cannot tell you about the quirks, characteristics and locations of individual winemakers, nor about their styles of vinification for the different grape varieties, especially since most of them make several different varieties. As an added complication, many of them are buying grapes from individual growers as well as using their own.

There is only one way to discover which styles you like: try them and compare. To find out which wines belong to which styles, you can read some of the books listed in the bibliography, ask friends and wine merchants and read newspapers and magazines. You will soon learn which wine writers and wine merchants' tastes coincide with yours, and as with all criticism, take note accordingly.

In any case, we can all learn what kinds of wines individual grapes make and what these will tend to taste like.

White Wines and Grapes

Today, white wine is much more popular in America than red wine is. It is lighter and generally more pleasing to drink without food. (The exceptions are the intentionally richly sweet white dessert wines.) White wine can be drunk younger than red wine, and therefore we are more likely to drink it at its peak. I still prefer red wine; but even for me there are unforgettably lovely white wines and meals which are happiest with white wine. While I like a cool white wine, I find that white wines are often served too cold in restaurants and in many homes. If the wine is too cold, we lose all the pleasures of perfume and all the subtleties of taste. A half hour of refrigeration before serving is plenty of time. On the other hand, if you find yourself with a white wine a little less good than you would like, serving it very cold will disguise its flaws.

Grapes from France

CHARDONNAY is without a doubt the grape whose wine has most proudly proclaimed California's splendor in the world forum. In France, Chardonnay is the wine grape of white Burgundy, but in blind tastings, even Frenchmen have often preferred a California Chardonnay to a famous Burgundy. Sometimes Chardonnay is mistakenly called Pinot Chardonnay, confusing it with a very different and less noble grape. It is not a Pinot at all.

In California, Chardonnay is vinified in two different ways. Both produce completely dry 100-percent varietals. Some of the grapes are picked early and vinified rapidly, and have little or no wood age on them. These wines tend to be lighter in color and make for less complicated drinking than the wines produced from fully ripened grapes and given a longer, slower vinification with a goodly amount of aging in French or other smallish oak casks. The latter are, consequently, deeper in color and flavor than the Chardonnays made by the first method.

All Chardonnays are described as big and

round rather than as fruity. The grapes are grown in almost every California area that has a claim to making fine wines and even in some that don't. So far, there is no particular correlation seen between growing area and style of vinification.

Chardonnays that are made for depth and complexity need more age—four to five years in the bottle—to round them out than do the lighter, clear wines. The light Chardonnays go well with light fish and seafood. The heavier ones do well with sauced fish and seafood, as well as with full-flavored birds and veal.

PINOT BLANC makes a simpler, fruitier, more acid wine than Chardonnay. In some parts of Burgundy it is blended with Chardonnay. In California, too, it is being used less and less as a separate varietal, but a great deal of it is being used to make California sparkling wine.

CHENIN BLANC is another wine grape with a nickname that confuses it with Chardonnay. It is sometimes called Pineau (*not* Pinot) de la Loire because it is one of the main grapes of the Loire Valley. There it produces lightly pleasant, slightly sweet, fruity wines. In California, it is sometimes vinified in the same way as in France, and at other times more austerely, with all the sugar being turned to alcohol and the wine aged in oak. I prefer this second vinification. I think Chenin Blanc has plenty of fruit and charm even when it is vinified absolutely dry.

Chenin Blanc is a wonderful wine to drink with the same foods that you couple with a Chardonnay. Select the Chenin Blanc when you want a more relaxed, gentle experience.

Chenin Blanc is also widely used in generic and brand-name whites.

SÉMILLON and SAUVIGNON BLANC are grapes that have similar problems in California. Both are grown in the Sauternes and Graves regions of France, where Sémillon is the major, and Sauvignon the blending, grape. In those areas, the wine from these grapes is almost invariably made very sweet. In many cases, the intensity of taste and sweetness comes from the natural appearance of *Botrytis* mold on the grapes. In California these grapes are made into both dry and sweet wines. Unfortunately, in neither case is there a name that clearly tells you whether the wine is dry or sweet. Some wine labels will help you by listing the residual sugar or describing the wine's characteristics on a back label.

Closely associated though these wines may be, they have very individual characteristics. Sauvignon Blanc has now become fairly popular under the name Fumé Blanc, coined for it by vineyard owner and winemaker Robert Mondavi. Although it is the less dominant of the two grapes in Sauternes, in California it seems to be the sturdier. Its nose, like green herbs after the rain on a spring morning, is assertive. The wine holds up well and can, in fact, use four to five years of bottle age. The problem with California sweet wines made from this grape is that *Botrytis* has not attacked the grapes to intensify the wine. Do not overchill these wines or you will lose much of their pleasurable fragrance.

Sémillon just doesn't become miraculous in California, either as a dry wine or as a sweet one. The rich, complex perfume—like that of a moist fig pudding—is too dense and intense for what turns out to be a light and uninteresting dry wine. As a sweet wine, it is still thin and one could kindly wish a plague of mold on both its houses.

FRENCH COLOMBARD was for many years the quintessential no-name grape. In recent years, it has become somewhat more visible. Originally planted in California to be a base for brandy, as it is in the Charente, Cognac's home district, it was found to make a good blending wine in the production of generics and brand-name wines. While it is still heavily used in these wines, it is beginning to peek shyly out as a varietal. As such it really doesn't resemble any European wine. When it is made with a hint of sweetness, it makes some people think of a Riesling. Made dry, it reminds some of a Macon. It is, rather, a good, clean, easily drinkable wine—a slightly upscale, all-purpose white with the advantage of being inexpensive.

Grapes from Germany and Alsace

German and Alsatian wines constitute a popular and attractive group, albeit with a confusion of nomenclature.

In Europe, these are the wines of cold-growing districts, districts where no good red wine grape grows. The more intense whites play the part there that reds play elsewhere. Also, because of the climate, the ordinary grapes do not develop much sugar, so the alcohol level of the wines is characteristically low. Sugar, when it does appear, is esteemed in its own right and for the roundness it gives the wines, permitting them to stand up to rich foods. Instead of vinifying all the sugar out to alcohol, some of the sugar is retained along with a rather low alcohol content.

In California's warmer climate, these wines are almost always more alcoholic than they are in Europe, and this decisively changes their character. In other parts of America, winemakers are trying these grapes with low alcohol in colder climates. A few resolute souls in California are also vinifying for low alcohol. This almost always results in a fairly sweet wine that may, in some cases, lack fruit acidity in the balance.

While there are many distinctions among the grapes in this group and among the wines made from them by vintners in different areas or with different styles, they have a common history as partners of meat and game. Some of the lighter members of the group are good picnic wines when chilled. The other, richer ones are best drunk with liver, curries, Chinese food and meat dishes made with cream, as well as with game, if you are not in the mood for an excellent red. The sweetest, botrytized versions are best served alone with dessert or instead of dessert. Some people enjoy these wines as accompaniments to sweetbread dishes, brains and—should you be so extravagant—foie gras.

GEWÜRTZTRAMINER, the first wine in this group, is the easiest to isolate and recognize. Although grown in the same areas and vinified in the same way as the Rieslings, it is a different species and has its own sharply pronounced character. The grape yields a spicy, fruity wine that tingles slightly on the tongue. Once you have smelled a Gewürtztraminer, you will always be able to recognize it. In Alsace, this grape's most important home, the wine, made bone dry, is rounded by its intense fruit. In California, some winemakers feel that the grape becomes bitter when vinified totally dry, perhaps as a result of the higher alcohol. These vintners therefore make their wines with an edge of sweetness that they feel conceals any bitterness. To me, the greatest weakness of the wine in this country is that the already powerful nose is made overwhelming by a high degree of alcohol; but there are people who are particularly attracted by this characteristic.

In any case, this wine is the perfect solution to the always difficult problem of what to serve with Oriental food. I even prefer it to beer, Champagne and whisky sours—the other good alcoholic partners of such food.

RIESLING is one of the most confusing words in California wine usage because it refers to so many grapes and so many wines, some of them not true Rieslings at all. In Germany, Riesling usually denotes the grape which in California is called White Riesling, Johannisberg Riesling, Rhine or German Riesling. In California, Riesling without a modifier generally refers to the Sylvaner or Franken Riesling grape. This grape, considered inferior in Alsace and Germany, is not a Riesling at all. Gray (or Grey) Riesling is an even more dubious appellation. The grape is not only not a Riesling, it is not even grown in the Riesling part of the world. It is also not very good.

Emerald Riesling looked promising when it was developed in California from a Riesling cross. Unfortunately, although the vine bears a large number of sturdy grapes and can be made into a clean, crisp wine, it is vastly less distinguished than its cousin, the true Riesling, and therefore has not grown much beyond the original plantings.

If you are interested in this style of wine, I think the true one, designated as White or Johannisberg, is by far the best. It is to me a feminine, elegant wine. In those rare cases where it has been made as a carefully, grape-by-grape selected, botrytized wine, it is one of the world's greatest, to be served only lightly chilled and drunk with respect. Fortunately, these wines, although expensive, are rich and a half bottle will suffice for a table of six.

Red Wines and Grapes

I am firmly on the red wine side. Given the choice, I will always drink the red rather than the white. If fish is the only food and the day is not too hot, I will drink red wine. If there are several courses in the meal, in the interest of diversity and the rhythm of the evening I will drink some white. However, I am peculiar. I don't move from dwelling to dwelling, and I believe in long-term relationships. Some of the most rewarding of these have been with my wines. To me, a 10-year-old wine, like a 10-year-old person, is a child and, while charming, less interesting to spend an evening with than a mature type.

Historically, red wine has been more expensive than white and more often drunk every day. This seems to conflict with current American reality, where much more white wine is being bought and drunk than red. There are many possible explanations for this apparent contradiction. It may be that in the past people drank more red wine because those areas of the world where wine grapes could be grown in profusion and inexpensively were regions that were so warm they could easily produce drinkable reds but had difficulty with comparably good whites.

Or perhaps it is because we have only recently become a wine-drinking nation, and white wines have less pronounced tastes than reds. Sweet reds are almost never good, for instance. Another reason may be that so far our white wines have been consistently better than our reds. Even more important is the fact that red wines tend to need more age in oak and in the bottle than whites, making the wines more expensive for the producer and for the public. We Americans do not yet have the habit of buying wines for the future and waiting for them to mature before we drink them. This means that we are certainly drinking red wines before their time, before they are fully balanced and delicious.

Another possible explanation is that Americans are eating more lightly, more frugally and with more concern for nutrition than ever before. To most people, white wines go better with less costly and less fattening foods than red wines, which are associated with red meat.

To enjoy red wines, we should remember that only at tastings are they drunk alone. They are born to go with food and do not taste their best without it. A big wine may overwhelm the taste buds without food; but drunk when eating, balanced by the natural fat and flavor of the food, it instantly smooths out, and its true virtues appear.

Incidentally, when people talk about drinking red wine at room temperature, they are talking about the temperature of rooms in big old stone houses—about 65 degrees F.—not American steam-heated rooms at 75 degrees.

To enjoy red wine at its best, use a largish glass and don't overfill it. Wine releases its aroma in contact with the air.

Which Red Wine?

California has produced an endless sea of red generic wine—a little soft, a little sweet—but the best red wines in the area, the varietals, have enormous character and rank with the world's finest. Some things are clear about some grapes. So far, the best red wines have been produced with the great red wine grapes of Bordeaux just as the whites have been made from the grapes of Burgundy. Similarly, a European style of vinification and aging in small oak barrels has brought out the best and biggest wines. While growers with lots of money tied up in inventory and drinkers eager to taste the new marvels may be impatient with high levels of tannin, it is essential for these big wines to show tannin for depth and oak for complexity.

Age and Vintage

Evidently, the age of the wine at drinking matters more for reds than for whites. The age the wine needs to be varies with the grape or grapes from which it is made, the style of the winemaker and

characteristics of the year—that is, the vintage—in which the grapes were grown. Bigger years, ones that develop more character in the grape, and bigger wines require more waiting. Years with too much rain at the wrong time yield thinner wines. While they may be attractive when young, they will not benefit from age and should be drunk early. Vintage charts are available and are updated, but they cannot tell about every individual wine. For specific information, ask your liquor store. If you want a wine that is ready to drink immediately, ask for it.

Blending

Another complication in learning about red wines is that they are often blended from the juice of several grapes. Many consumers believe that if a wine is made from only one grape variety it is better. This is not true. In Bordeaux—from which we get California's most successful red wine grape, Cabernet Sauvignon—the predominant grape is blended with Cabernet Franc, Malbec or Merlot, depending on the characteristics of the year and the tradition of the winemaker. Nobody thinks of this blending as wrong. Usually they do not think about it at all; the wines are named after the estates or pieces of ground where they are made instead of after the grapes. Increasingly, California winemakers are discovering the subtleties of blending. Occasionally, the grape percentages are listed on the labels. In any case, it is the character of the predominant grape that will be most marked in the wine. The other grapes are blended in for taste and balance.

Grapes from France

CABERNET SAUVIGNON is the hands-down winner to date in the California red wine sweepstakes. Unfortunately, it is difficult to find the older, mature wines because so few of them were made and those in small quantities. In 1960, slightly more than 600 acres were planted with this grape; today there are over 25,000 acres. If you can find an older wine, even six or seven years old, from a good winery, it will be worth the search. If you really like wine or think you might enjoy big wines in the future, each year buy a case or more of a good Cabernet, put it in a cool, dark place with a fairly even temperature, and leave it alone for a few years; it will repay your patience with superior drinking. You can shorten the waiting time by looking for somewhat older bottles.

Cabernet is one of the hardest wines to describe. It has a complex perfume and taste that are its glory. It is variously described as herbaceous (more spring grass than cooking herbs, I think), like green olives or like currants. It should not taste like raisins or prunes—an indication that the wine is either over-age or not made from good grapes in the first place. To me, Cabernet is like nothing so much as Cabernet, and it is worth learning to identify.

Big Cabernets go splendidly with lamb and steak. Elegant ones bring out the best in sauced dishes and, if you like red with birds as I do, in duck and other full-flavored birds. Of course, elegant and big are not necessarily in conflict. When you get them together, you have the best of all possible worlds, and a good piece of cheese will be the best homage.

CABERNET FRANC is almost never made as a varietal on its own. It is a grape that seems to modify the taste of Cabernet Sauvignon very little and yet, when combined with it, makes the wine ready to drink earlier.

MALBEC is another grape that is used mainly for blending with Cabernets. It gives a richness and heaviness to wines in which it is used.

MERLOT is also a grape used for blending with Cabernet, but it is well worth attending to on its own. Almost all the great Cabernets of France and many of those of California are improved by the velvety roundness of Merlot. As a varietal, Merlot is ready to drink earlier than Cabernet. It tends to make voluptuous and seductive wine, somewhat less aristocratic than Cabernet but meant to be drunk with the same foods.

PINOT NOIR is the wine grape of Burgundy, as Cabernet is that of Bordeaux. After that the parallel stops. Pinot Noir has neither the success nor the taste in California that is has in Burgundy. In California it makes a lighter, less impressive wine that is drunk much younger than its European counterparts. And yet . . . I have faith. I believe that we are just beginning to see what Pinot Noir can do in California. Some of the newer wines are starting to show that wonderful fruity nose, like ripe raspberries, that is characteristic of great Pinot Noir. Perhaps the rich depth of taste will follow.

While Pinot Noir may be waiting to show its stuff as a red wine in California, it is already doing a fabulous job as a lightly tinted rosé, confusingly called Blanc de Pinot Noir, or white Pinot Noir, and as an important grape for the making of sparkling wines.

GAMAY is the name for two unrelated grapes in California. Much more confusing than that you really cannot get. The first grape, Gamay Beaujolais, is really a clone of Pinot Noir. The other, usually called Napa Gamay or just Gamay, is the grape from which Beaujolais-district wines are made in France. The confusion is the result of a previous case of mistaken identity. If you want a wine for young drinking that has a flowery nose and a light, fruity taste, you want the Napa Gamay. Beaujolais will also be light but will lack the fruit and flowers.

These wines are best drunk lightly chilled and informally, with hearty foods. If you are used to French Beaujolais, however, watch for the higher alcohol content of these wines from California's sunnier climate.

SYRAH, the grape of the big wines of the Côtes du Rhône, is just beginning to get a trial in California. In those few instances, it is making big, full-flavored wines with a great deal of style, if not elegance. These are wines to drink with direct food and without too much aging.

PETITE SYRAH is another case of mistaken identity; for many years it was thought to be the grape described above. It makes a rather simple, if heavy, direct wine and is clearly recognizable in the many jug wines in which it is used. It is not a wine of which I am overly fond.

The Mediterranean Grape

CARIGNANE is the red wine grape that is virtually never named. It is the biggest producer in the jug/table wine field. It is coarse, jolly and without much distinction, like the red wines from the south of France that are also made with this grape. Carignane makes an ideal pasta-with-tomato-sauce wine.

The American Grape

ZINFANDEL must have come from somewhere, and in recent years there have been attempts to locate its ancestors in the south of Italy. But no matter where it comes from, it is the most Californian of all our wines. When I have European guests, I invariably serve them a well-made Zinfandel. I find that they respect the qualities of the wine and, since there is no directly comparable European wine, they are spared defensive comparisons.

Zinfandel grows easily in every wine-growing area of California and has been made into wines of as many different styles as there are vineyards. Two styles I can get out of the way quickly by saying that I just plain don't think they are any good. These are white Zinfandels and Late Harvest Zinfandels. The whites have no freshness to recommend them. The Late Harvests have as much alcohol as port, although by some alchemy it is arrived at by fermentation without the level of alcohol killing the yeast. The trouble is that the hyper-mature grapes used to make these wines cause the wines to taste of raisins.

There are very good Zinfandels being made, and they seem to fall into two basic categories. One category is that of fresh, fruity wines without too much tannin, made to be drunk young. The other category includes more austere and tannic wines made somewhat like Bordeaux and meant to be drunk with several mellowing years of age on them. I very much enjoy both of these styles of wine when they are well made. While Zinfandel will probably never achieve the elegance of a really fine Cabernet, many Zinfandels are at a generally fine level and make pleasant companions for regular mealtime drinking.

Grapes from Italy

It is amazing that, given the number of wine-makers in California who are of Italian descent, there are not more Italian grape varieties planted in the state. What is more, the wines made from the two varieties that have been planted in any quantity have generally been thin, light wines without much distinction. This seems a pity and tends to obscure the few times when the grapes have been used to make better wines.

BARBERA is originally from the Piedmont. In California, as in Italy, it makes at its best a gutsy wine ready to stand up to game and other rich foods. At its worst it is simply rough and thin.

NEBBIOLO, a yet finer grape from the Piedmont, has had even less success in California. There are hopes for the future but no present success.

The Rosé Wine Grapes

To tell the truth, there is really only one rosé wine grape, and that is Grenache. Wherever this red-skinned grape is planted it is good for only one thing, and that is to make rosé. I think that there are better rosés. The best ones come from the great red wine grapes, Cabernet and Pinot Noir. They are fruity, elegant and light with an edge of complexity and a balanced fruit acidity.

Normally, I do not drink rosé at all. I don't think it is the wine that goes with everything, but rather the wine that goes with nothing. I have had to learn new habits for the very elegant California rosés (generally not called rosés at all but disguising themselves as whites). Whatever their names, they tend to be excellent buys and excellent wines. They are lighter than the big Chardonnays, fruitier and more seductive. At the same time they are more elegant than most of the Chenin Blancs. They are often the best California wine to use in the place of a chilled Beaujolais.

Sparkling Wines

These are the only wines in California that, at their finest, still go under the name of the European generic: Champagne. They are rarely defined by their grape variety. I think this is too bad, for California bubbly is very, very good and does not have to pass itself off as anything else.

California sparkling wines are categorized in three ways: by the color of the grape from which they are made, by sweetness, and by whether or not they have been finished at the end in the way that French Champagnes are—with a dose of brandy and sugar. This dose, incidentally, is true even of the classically driest, "brut" wines.

Although we tend to think of good sparkling wines as white, this is only a prejudice brought on by the overabundance of bad pink bubbly. It is the quality of the grapes and the quality of the winemaker that make the difference.

Perhaps in these wines more than in any other it is a good thing to find out which companies make a wine you like and go back to it. This is because sparkling wines are usually blends not only of different grape varieties but also of grapes from different growing areas and years in order to achieve a standardized taste that is house-style.

To me the best of the sparkling wines are those made in the true Champagne method: that is, fermented in the bottle, thus trapping in the yeasty bubbles. I particularly like the pinkish Blanc de Pinot Noir and the Blanc from Gamay. These are full-bodied wines that give a festive lift to any evening or luxurious summer afternoon. If you prefer a sharper, lighter sparkling wine, try the white ones made from white grapes.

I don't think there is much point in trying to save money on these wines. Good sparkling wines are rather costly to produce, with a lot of hand-turning of the bottles so that the sediment from the in-bottle fermentation comes to rest on the cork and can be miraculously and deftly removed without letting out the bubbles. This means that what you pay for is what you get, and a bad sparkling wine can send everybody back to beer in a minute. As to sweetness, that is a matter of taste and where in the meal you plan to serve your bubbly. The most expensive and prestigious Champagnes and sparkling wines have been the "brut" or very dry ones. Those labelled "dry" are actually slightly sweet and should be drunk with dessert if you like but not before a meal or at a reception.

California Wine-Producing Regions

There are basically two jobs in the making of wine: growing the grapes and making the grapes into wine. Sometimes, in California as elsewhere, the two jobs are performed by the same person or company; sometimes these are two separate functions, with the winemaker buying grapes from the vineyard owner; and sometimes the wine producer buys crushed grapes or juice.

All these possible variations make it hard to know exactly where a wine comes from unless you read the label very carefully. If the label says Napa Valley Chardonnay, you know that at least 75 percent of the grapes used to make the wine—Chardonnay or not—must come from Napa Valley. However, if the address of the winery is simply given as Napa Valley without specifically referring to the grape, the grapes can come from anywhere in California. Also, climate and soil can vary from one part of a growing region to another; therefore a winemaker at one end of Sonoma Valley who buys grapes or has vineyards at the other end of Sonoma is telling you *something* when he says he is making a Sonoma Valley wine, but it is not very precise. The best labels give a fairly exact growing location or vineyard name.

San Francisco Bay and city are in northern California. Try to imagine San Francisco as the knot at the center of a bow whose two loops extend north and south. Think of the undulations in the loops radiating from the knot as a series of mountain ranges and valleys, and you have the California wine-growing areas.

North of San Francisco

The two most prestigious growing areas in California lie to the north of San Francisco. One is known, vaguely, as Sonoma and the other, precisely, as Napa. They are physically defined by ridges of mountains running northward from San Francisco, parallel to the Pacific coast.

Sonoma falls into two counties and many more growing areas than Napa. Starting at the cool southern end near San Francisco, there is Carneros, the remains of an extensive wine-growing world. The pressure of San Francisco's population has left wineries there but virtually no vines. Going north, one comes to Sonoma Valley proper, also called the Valley of the Moon. Just north of the designated Sonoma Valley area lies the Russian River. Having originated farther north in Mendocino County, it perversely turns west halfway through Sonoma County and finds an exit to the ocean instead of proceeding, as one might expect, in an orderly fashion to the bay. It is the course of the Russian River that organizes the growing areas in the northern section of Sonoma. They are Russian River Valley, Alexander Valley and Dry Creek Valley.

Farther north still is an area that used to be considered a part of Sonoma but is now seen as having its own identity. The area is in Mendocino County, and its wines are variously labeled as growing regions: Mendocino, Ukiah and Anderson Valley—also organized by the Russian River. While Sonoma and Mendocino are still defining themselves, so far their best wines have been reds, and among those the Zinfandels and Cabernets.

Across the ridge of the Mayacamas Mountains from this loosely defined Sonoma area is Napa, which is both a county and a valley. Until recently, for wine purposes, the county and the valley were deemed to be synonymous, even though there are vineyards perched perilously up in the steep hills and the climate varies markedly in different parts of the valley. Gradually, names for smaller divisions are coming into general usage. Generally they are the names of towns and indicate the land in the immediate area. Napa starts, as does Sonoma, cool in the south, in the Carneros region, and makes its way warmly north.

The winemakers of Napa got a jump on the rest of California in making fine varietals in the postwar period. Napa has developed a fine reputation not only for the most important of these—Cabernet, Chardonnay, Zinfandel, White Riesling and Pinot Noir—but also for sparkling wines made from the superb valley grapes and for adventurous small vineyard productions.

South of San Francisco

South of San Francisco there are basically two important grape-growing and wine-producing areas. One is what is called the North Coast, running down into the Central Coast. Romantic as this sounds, the vines do not overlook the ocean but are protected, as are the growing areas north of San Francisco, by a coastal mountain chain. Some of the vines are planted on the inland, valley-facing sides of these slopes, and some in the valley itself. One of the better known regional designations here is that of one of the major counties, Monterey. The area is somewhat new to the fine varietal wine business. Monterey seems to do best with the white grapes, adding a little muscle and pleasant acid to the wines. So far, these additions do not do much for red wines. The northern part of this valley does well with Zinfandels.

To the east of San Francisco Bay, the Livermore Valley grapes have become virtually an endangered species as the subdivisions of the East Bay cities encroach on the vineyards.

The next valley inward and southward is the largest producing area of California, the San Joaquin Valley, which blankets the better part of five counties. Its wines are not the finest—the mysterious jugs and table wines come from here. The largest wine-producing companies in America call this valley home. In recent years, as the American palate has become sophisticated, the valley growers and producers have been upgrading their grapes. They have also developed new ways to prune the vines so as to provide shade for the grapes, and they have begun to mist the vineyards in order to bring the temperature down. All in all, we are seeing better wines from better grapes.

There are other small areas of grape growing farther south in California. Some are in San Luis Obispo County, particularly around the town of Paso Robles. This area produced badly made wine for years. Now, some very good winemakers have settled down to make very worthwhile red varietals. Some are around Santa Barbara, and the new wineries in this area are producing some surprisingly good wines, worth looking at for the future. Farther south still, near Los Angeles, there are vineyards and wineries with deeply convinced owners but the results to date have been extremely spotty.

Whatever districts they come from, whatever grapes are used, whatever the vinification style, the wines of California are coming along splendidly. They are enriching our daily lives and adding excitement to our special moments. What we cook tastes better coupled with these wines.

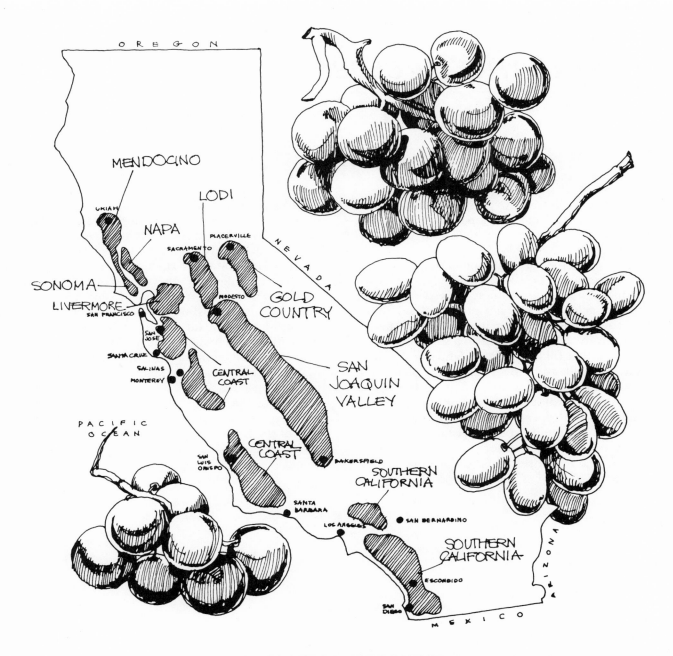

THE CALIFORNIA WINE COUNTRY

About the Recipes

Cooking is intensely personal, and so the recipes I give reflect me. I hope they will become foundations for your own ideas and your own recipes.

At best, recipes are only indications of how a dish tastes when I cook it. Inevitably, one lemon has more juice than another, is sweeter, fruitier or more acid. You will have to taste and adjust to accommodate your own ingredients and tastes.

Generally, what I look for in a soup or a sauce is a taste that fills my mouth lightly or emphatically, giving pleasure to all the sensors on my lips, tongue and palate. I want an appropriate scent, not a stench. I want a plate, pot or platter to look beautiful. That does not mean artificial or attitudinized. I don't like roses or potato baskets not meant to be eaten. I abhor gratuitous sprigs of parsley; the food itself must seduce me.

I like food with a definite taste and point of view. I like the sharp, light zing of lemon juice and use a lot of it, particularly when I must content myself with canned tomatoes or fruits in a less than ideal state of ripeness. The acid in the fruit does not develop unless the fruit ripens naturally. Without the addition of acid the fruit taste and the sugar both seem less intense.

I still love salt. Nature has gifted and cursed me with a low metabolism. If you are used to little or no salt, eliminate it from the recipe. You may want to increase the spices and acids slightly to compensate.

Many of the recipes call for stock and glazes because I like their flavors. You may want to look at the Basic Recipes section for some emergency solutions or substitute good canned stocks.

Recipes

FIRST COURSES

I often feel that the best—and quickest—first course is a little smoked salmon or trout, a summer salad of sliced tomatoes with basil and a light dressing, or a few barely cooked stalks of asparagus with a little melted butter. However, there are occasions that require more.

Frequently, the best wine solution is to continue serving the not-too-heavy white your guests have been drinking before dinner or to start the wine you are going to serve with the main course. Nevertheless, I have given you some special ideas for wine to serve with each recipe. If you have a sizable group of guests it is not more expensive to serve two different wines than the same number of bottles of one wine. Sometimes it will be less expensive, as the opening white may cost less. Two wines are certainly more festive, and the table looks beautiful set with two glasses at each place.

Smoked Salmon Mousse
Serves 10 to 12

This is one of my favorite first courses, and I have never served it to less than rave reviews. It is based on a mousse I ate at Jacques Cagna's extraordinary restaurant in Paris. He does not add any gelatin to his mousse and serves it softly spoon-molded. Both versions are delicious, but I think there is something dramatic about bringing the whole salmon-pink mold to the table. Even a medium-sized stainless steel bowl will serve well as a mold. In the interest of contrast in color, texture and taste, I have added the crisp, lightly onion-greenness of chives.

Why is this American? Because one of the great natural bounties of the American land is its salmon.

The early settlers found the Indians smoking or cooking sides of salmon on tilted boards propped up around a fire. Today much of the salmon smoked in Scotland actually originates in Canada and the United States.

Today's salmon, no matter where it comes from, is more delicate in flavor and fatter than it used to be. This is because we now refrigerate it instead of depending on salt, smoke and dryness to preserve the fish. Nevertheless, the taste and saltiness of the salmon you buy will vary from fish to fish. Be sure to taste your mixture before adding salt and adjust the lemon juice accordingly.

Wonderful as food processors are, there is no way to avoid sieving this mixture or it will feel gritty.

This is a relatively economical though festive dish, since a very little smoked salmon will serve a fairly large number of people. Any fabulous or merely delightful wine will be shown to advantage by the delicate taste and voluptuous fat of this dish. Try a very good Chardonnay which has acquired several years of rounding bottle age, a delicately dry Johannisberg Riesling with a perfume of spring or, when economizing, a dry white jug wine.

3 tablespoons water
1 package (¼ ounce) unflavored gelatin
6½ ounces Nova Scotia smoked salmon
3 cups heavy cream
2 tablespoons fresh lemon juice
2½ teaspoons grated onion
2 teaspoons kosher salt
Freshly ground white pepper
10 drops Tabasco sauce
¼ cup sliced chives

GARNISH:
Thin chives
Smoked salmon (optional)

Oil 10 ½-cup molds, a 5-cup mold or a 1-quart mold for service and a small mold for the cook and set aside.

Place the water in a small pan. Add the gelatin and let it sit until absorbed. Place the pan over low heat and stir until the gelatin is dissolved. Set aside to cool to room temperature.

Put the smoked salmon and ½ cup heavy cream in a food processor and process until smooth. Then press the mixture through a fine sieve to give you a smooth puree.

Whip the remaining 2½ cups cream just until slightly soft peaks form. Beat in the dissolved gelatin. Stir in the lemon juice, onion, salt, pepper, Tabasco and chives.

Remove about ½ cup of the seasoned whipped cream and stir it into the sieved smoked salmon to lighten the mixture. Fold in the remaining cream. Spoon into the prepared mold or molds. Refrigerate 1½ hours, or until set.

To serve, unmold and garnish with additional chives and smoked salmon, if desired.

Watercress Mousse with Raw Ham

Watercress, grown in such profusion in our South, is too scrumptious to use only as a soup ingredient or as a garnish for a plate of steak. Here its peppery freshness gives its all to a light mousse to be served with thin, raw slices of Smithfield ham. Too often we have heard Italian cooks in America bemoan the absence of the true Parma prosciutto. Smithfield ham, thinly shaved, is quite different but every bit as good. Shaved ham and baking powder biscuits are a classic Southern picnic treat. I myself use Vermont corncob-smoked ham.

With this you could serve a cold and spicy California Gewürztraminer.

3 bunches watercress, washed
1¼ cups heavy cream
3 egg yolks
½ plus ⅛ teaspoon kosher salt
Generous amount freshly ground
**   white pepper**
Pinch ground red pepper
6 thin slices raw Smithfield or
**   Vermont country ham**

Heat the oven to 325 degrees. Bring a large pot of salted water to a boil. Lightly grease 6 ¼-cup ceramic molds. Set aside.

Remove the leaves from the stems of the watercress. Reserve the leaves and a packed cup of stems. Discard the remaining stems. Plunge the watercress leaves into the boiling water and boil for 6 minutes, to intensify the flavor and color while softening the leaves.

Drain the leaves in a sieve and rinse immediately under cold running water. Squeeze the leaves dry with your hands, then wrap them in a kitchen towel and squeeze dry.

Coarsely chop the cup of reserved stems. Put them into a small saucepan with 1 cup heavy cream. Bring to a boil; reduce the heat and simmer for 10 minutes. Strain and reserve the cream, discarding the stems.

Put the dry watercress leaves in the work bowl of a food processor with the remaining ¼ cup cream. Process just un-

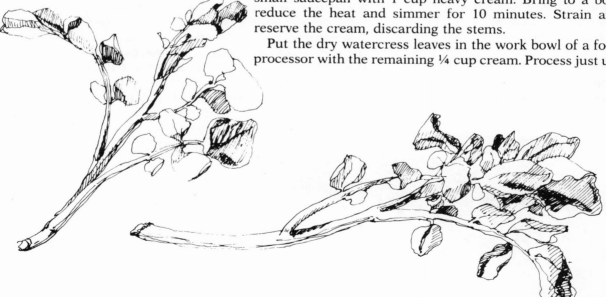

til the watercress is finely chopped. Add the contents of the bowl to the simmered cream.

Force the entire mixture through a sieve into a mixing bowl. Add the egg yolks, salt and peppers.

Divide the mixture among the greased molds. Place them in a baking dish and add hot water to come halfway up the sides of the molds. Bake in the preheated oven for 25 to 30 minutes, or until set. Remove from the baking dish and cool slightly on a rack, then refrigerate for at least 4 hours.

To serve, unmold onto individual serving plates and garnish with the raw ham.

Buckwheat Noodles with Golden American Caviar and Lemon Beurre Blanc

Serves 4

This is a recipe that borrows from all over to make a new American dish. It all started with a wonderful new caviar from California that has moderately small, well-formed eggs and is entrancingly pale apricot-gold. Upon tasting, the eggs turn out to be firm, not tough, and as elegant in flavor as they are in appearance. The caviar is made from the roe of whitefish from the Great Lakes and is not artificially colored.

I felt that a new dish had to be created for this new star. This dish combines a noodle that echoes the traditional affinity of blini—Russia's yeasty buckwheat pancakes—and caviar.

Fortunately, the caviar is inexpensive, particularly when used in the rather small quantities needed for this recipe. The caviar keeps well frozen, so you can always have it on hand.

The dough is one of the most sensual I have ever felt, soft and slightly powdery like a baby's bottom. With an Italian pasta machine, it is easy to work. Incidentally, I use beer as the liquid to intensify the yeast taste. The dough becomes difficult to roll if the yeast alone provides the flavor and the dough is allowed to rise too long.

The natural drink with this first course is a good bubbly. A Chardonnay of weight and authority would be a good alternative.

½ cup beer, at room temperature
1 teaspoon dry yeast
¼ cup buckwheat flour
1 cup all-purpose flour
¼ teaspoon kosher salt

In a small bowl, combine ¼ cup beer, the yeast and 2 tablespoons buckwheat flour. Cover and let rise in a warm place for at least 1 hour.

Stir in the remaining 2 tablespoons buckwheat flour, the all-purpose flour, salt and enough beer to make a soft but firm dough. Cover the dough loosely and let rest for about 20 to 30 minutes.

Divide the dough into 4 pieces. Using a pasta machine, begin to roll out the dough, a piece at a time, beginning at the widest opening and working to the second or third thinnest. If, as you work, the dough seems sticky, lightly flour it.

Hang the dough up to dry slightly. Repeat with the remaining pieces. Take the first strip and cut it for fettuccine. Toss the cut noodles with a small amount of all-purpose flour. Repeat with the remaining sheets of pasta.

Cook the pasta in abundant boiling salted water until barely tender. Drain thoroughly.

LEMON BEURRE BLANC

½ cup plus 1 teaspoon fresh lemon
   juice
½ pound unsalted butter, cut into
   ½-inch pieces, kept cold
2 tablespoons golden American caviar

Pour ½ cup lemon juice into a heavy non-aluminum saucepan and cook until reduced to a glaze—about 1 tablespoon. Remove the pan from the heat and touch the bottom. It should be just hot enough to permit you to withstand the heat for a second or two. Quickly whisk in 2 pieces of butter. When it is soft and creamy but not melted, whisk in more butter. As the pan cools, it will be necessary to return it to a low heat. As it gets hot, remove it again. Continue in this way as you whisk in the butter, 2 pieces at a time. You are not really melting the butter but frothing it and making an emulsion with the acid.

When all the butter has been added and absorbed, add the remaining teaspoon lemon juice. Taste. Off the heat, stir in 1 tablespoon caviar.

When both sauce and pasta are ready, spoon about 2 tablespoons of the sauce into each of 4 salad plates. Over that, mound equal portions of the cooked pasta. Divide the remaining sauce among the plates and spoon over the pasta. Top each mound of pasta with a fourth of the remaining tablespoon caviar.

Shad Roe Soufflé with String Bean Frappé   *Serves 6*

Every spring eastern American rivers swarm with shad going upstream to spawn. The unfertilized eggs, or roe, are a reliable sign of the season.

Poaching roe whole in an enveloping bath of melted butter is one of the best ways of cooking it. For something a little more spectacular, try this barely risen unmolded soufflé turned out onto a bed of cool, green string-bean sauce. The beans are less competitive and assertive than the usual sorrel—and also easier to come by.

However, perusal of an herb book will teach you how to recognize sorrel's shield-shaped leaves. The nearest patch of weeds or untidy lawn should yield you a handful of wild sorrel, more flavorful and more tender by far than the French or domesticated variety. To prepare a simple sorrel sauce, cut the leaves across the vein into thin strips—a chiffonade. Melt about 1 cup of packed strips in 1 tablespoon of butter in a non-aluminum pan. Cook with ½ cup heavy cream for 5 minutes. Bind with the yolk of 1 egg.

The green-bean sauce will cause less trouble with the wine since it does not have the sharp acid of sorrel. A simple, easy white with some body, such as a French Colombard or a Sémillon, will be pleasant.

3 tablespoons unsalted butter
2 pairs (approximately 12 ounces total) shad roe
4 large eggs, separated
¾ cup heavy cream
2 teaspoons fresh lemon juice
1 teaspoon kosher salt
⅛ teaspoon freshly ground black pepper

Heat the oven to 350 degrees. Butter and flour 6 ¾-cup ramekins. Set aside.

Melt the butter in a skillet over low heat. Add the roe in a single layer and cook gently for 2 to 3 minutes on each side. Do not overcook.

Put the roe through a ricer; discard the skin. Beat the egg yolks, cream, lemon juice, salt and pepper into the roe.

In a clean bowl, beat the whites until stiff. Fold them into the roe mixture. Divide evenly among the prepared ramekins. Place in a baking pan; add hot water to come halfway up the sides of the molds. Bake in the preheated oven for 20 minutes, or until set.

While still warm, unmold onto individual plates. Surround with String Bean Frappé.

NOTE: If you wish to serve this as a main course at lunch, use 4 3½-inch ceramic quiche molds.

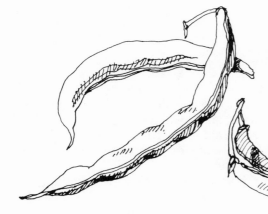

STRING BEAN FRAPPÉ

1½ pounds string beans, boiled until tender, then refreshed under cold water
Kosher salt
Freshly ground black pepper
¼ cup olive oil

Puree the beans in a food processor until smooth. Force the mixture through a fine sieve. Add salt and pepper to taste, then the olive oil.

Serve immediately.

SOUPS

I love soup. I like to eat it and I like to cook it. It is related to the cooking of stews and sauces—other favorites of mine. Aside from impeccable consommés which have to be clarified to within an inch of their lives, soups are forgiving. A little too much this, a little too little that, will not be a disaster. Cold soups are not only welcome to the eater in summer, they are also an aid to the cook, since they can be left happily in the refrigerator until just before service. While there are many cold cream soups, I frankly favor the clear soups—jellied or frozen.

However, soups are often a problem when planning a meal to be accompanied by wine or organized around wine. The coward's solution is not to serve wine at all. I always think that is a mistake. It causes a sudden lull in spirits after people have been festively having a drink before dinner.

If you have been serving a light white wine such as Johannisberg Riesling or a Chenin Blanc before dinner, continue it with the soup. If you are just starting wine, consider one of the roses or apricot-colored wines that are now coming from California, sometimes mysteriously labeled as Blanc de Pinot Noir. If you are going to serve a simple red, lightly chilled, such as a Napa Gamay or a Gamay Beaujolais, with the main course, start it with the soup. With something as liquid as soup, a half bottle will often be enough for four people. Do have wine.

Incidentally, when the urgent desire for soup hits me on a hot summer day, I often cheat by using canned chicken stock instead of my homemade version. Then I have to be careful about salt since my stock is unseasoned and canned stock is almost always salted.

Fresh Tomato and Chicken Soup

Aromatic and fresh, this soup depends on impeccable tomatoes, rich with flavor. Like most of these soups, it is equally elegant served cold the following day. In that case, do not add the final butter.

2 quarts chicken stock (see Basic Recipes)
4½ pounds fresh, ripe tomatoes, cored and roughly chopped
11 large basil leaves
3 sprigs fresh lovage
5 sprigs Italian parsley
2 tablespoons fresh dill cut into ¼-inch pieces
1½ teaspoons (approximate) kosher salt
Unsalted butter

Place the stock, tomatoes, basil, lovage and parsley in a stainless steel pot. Cover and bring to a boil. Remove the cover, lower the heat until the mixture simmers and continue to cook until the tomatoes are very soft.

Put the mixture through the fine blade of a food mill, or chop in a food processor and then push through a sieve. Return to the pot.

Add the dill and cook 20 minutes longer. Season to taste with salt.

For each serving, place a lump of butter in the bowl and ladle hot soup over.

NOTES: If fresh lovage is not available, substitute celery leaves and increase the amount of basil and dill. If your tomatoes are watery, use more tomatoes and less stock. The soup may be made ahead through the sieving. Chill, then finish the soup just before serving.

Bourbon Corn Chowder

Serves 6

Many Chinese restaurants use canned creamed corn in their soups. I have found that it works very well in this chowder. You can, of course, use fresh corn scraped off the cob. But if you do use the canned corn and have on hand either canned or homemade chicken stock, I think you will find this a delicious—and quick—soup. It is the kind of soup that can be lunch if served in a large bowl with a salad and dessert.

4 tablespoons unsalted butter
¾ cup chopped onion
2½ cups canned creamed corn
¼ cup bourbon
¼ teaspoon grated nutmeg
1 teaspoon kosher salt
Freshly ground black pepper
2 to 3 drops Tabasco sauce
½ cup chicken stock (see Basic Recipes)
½ cup heavy cream

Melt the butter in a saucepan. Add the onion and cook until transparent. Stir in the corn.

Heat the bourbon in a small pan. Ignite the alcohol and let it flame for 1 minute. Pour the bourbon, still flaming, over the corn mixture. Stir in the remaining ingredients. Heat thoroughly and serve hot.

NOTE: If you prefer a thinner soup, add more stock.

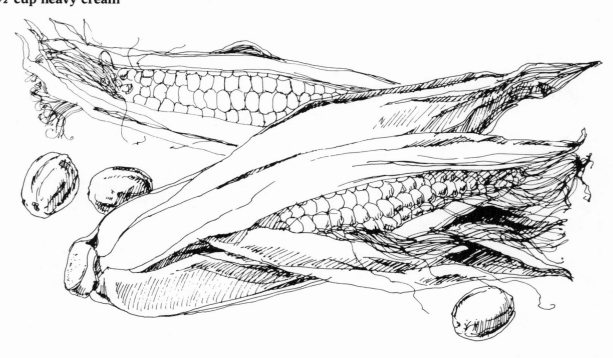

Turkey Soup with Quenelles and Egg Noodles

Serves 10 to 12

I am one of those who often cooks turkey in order to have bones and carcass for turkey soup. Incidentally, when I clear the plates, I save the bones; the cooking of stock will boil away anything unhygienic. Basically, turkey soup requires nothing but a little salt and some rice or noodles. However, it is so good that I sometimes dress it up for company. I made this version for James Beard's birthday, and it was well received.

At a festive dinner, this soup can superbly hold its own with a light, dry Johannisberg Riesling.

½ **pound skinned and boned turkey breast, cut into 1-inch cubes**
2 **egg whites**
1 **cup heavy cream**
2 **tablespoons fresh chives**
2 **tablespoons fresh tarragon**
3½ **quarts turkey stock (see Basic Recipes)**
Kosher salt
1 **teaspoon cayenne pepper**
½ **pound egg noodles**

Place the turkey in a food processor and process until smooth. Add the egg whites and continue processing. With the machine running, pour in the cream and process another minute.

Add the chives and tarragon and process for 1 to 2 minutes, or until the herbs are well chopped.

Press the mixture through a medium-fine sieve into a clean bowl. Chill until ready to cook.

Bring the stock to a boil and season to taste with salt and cayenne. Add salt slowly and taste carefully; you will find that even a full-flavored stock can benefit from the addition of some salt.

Meanwhile, cook the egg noodles in salted water until just barely done. Drain and keep warm.

Lower the heat so the stock simmers. Using 2 wet teaspoons, form the turkey puree into smooth ovals and drop them into the simmering stock. Let cook for no more than 2 minutes.

Serve the soup in bowls with the noodles, making sure that each serving has several turkey quenelles.

Peapod Soup

While I love fresh peas in spring and summer, after I shell them there always seem to be many more pods than peas. My thrifty and lazy soul revolts at throwing them out. With just a little extra effort, they can be turned into a delicious and subtle soup. Though it tastes gently of peas, it also tastes as if there were a mystery ingredient.

2 pounds fresh peas, in the pod
6 cups chicken stock (see Basic
   Recipes)
2 egg yolks
½ cup heavy cream
Kosher salt
Freshly ground black pepper

Shell the peas by pulling the strings. Discard the tips and strings of the pods. Reserve the peas for another use. Bring the stock to a boil and add the pods, stirring them in well to immerse them. Reduce the heat to a low boil and cook for 45 minutes, or until the pods are extremely tender. Remove from the heat.

In two or three batches, puree the pods and stock in a food processor. Return the puree to the saucepan and heat.

In a small dish, beat the egg yolks lightly with the cream. Stirring constantly, pour about 1 cup of the hot soup into the egg-cream mixture to temper it. Stir this mixture into the soup. Cook over medium heat, stirring constantly, until the soup thickens slightly and coats the back of the spoon. Adjust the seasoning to taste with salt and pepper.

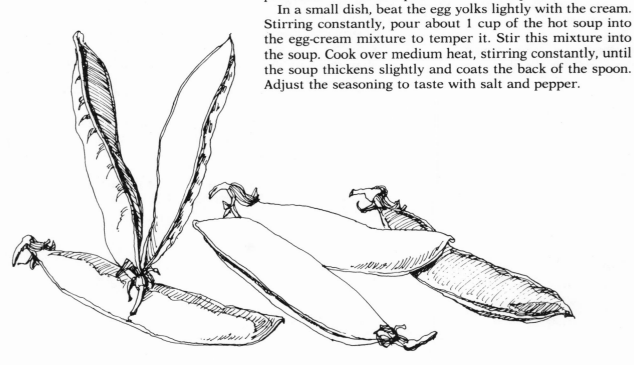

POULTRY

All over America we raise chickens. American chickens, however, are constantly being insulted by the press. It is true that free-range chickens with complex flavors are few and far between—almost as rare as hens of a certain age for making a decent soup. We do have an abundant supply of relatively inexpensive birds providing a good source of protein and, if the skin is removed, few calories. Our young chickens are also a godsend in that they cook quickly. In fact their major flaw is that they are generally overcooked. With a little imagination on the part of the cook, the chickens are an enormous resource. I often add a little chicken glaze to intensify the chicken flavor. The directions for making the glaze can be found in the section covering Basic Recipes.

Ducks—brought from China—used to be the specialty of Long Island. Now new breeds are being raised in California and elsewhere. These Muscovy and other new ducks have less fat under the skin than usually available ducks. They also have heavier breasts with more blood. They are very good in recipes calling for duck breasts.

Most Americans eat their duck for the crisped skin, as do fanciers of Peking duck. The Czechs and Viennese are also crisp-skin enthusiasts. The French and Italians tend to ignore or even remove the skin in honor of the richer, moister flesh.

Turkey seems to be the quintessentially American bird. Indeed, there was a long campaign to make the scrawny-necked wild beast our national bird instead of the noble-looking but predatory bald eagle. Wild turkey is available to few of us, but the domesticated bird seems to be requisite for every important holiday. We also now have disembodied breasts available frozen or otherwise processed. (I often wonder what they do with all those legs.) I recommend looking for small, whole turkeys that have not been chemically tampered with. I made a comparative test cooking both the treated breast and the fresh, unadulterated turkey meat. The results were much as you might imagine, but now I can have my say with certainty rather than expressing a prejudice. If your turkey breast meat is dried out, it simply means that you have cooked the turkey at too low a temperature for too long.

Never refrigerate the cooked bird if you can avoid it unless it is immersed in a sauce. The extensive gelatin in the meat stiffens, and no amount of letting the bird come back to room temperature will give you anything but cardboard.

Incidentally, it is illegal in most states to sell just the duck and chicken feet called for in many traditional soup recipes; but if you can locate a good Chinese poultry market it will sell both creatures with feet attached. Lop them off, freeze them, and save them for soup-making day.

I am a red wine lover and will—when a choice is marginally possible—always pick the red wine. With fowl, it's almost always red. I'll even serve a cold chicken on a hot day with a chilled, undemanding red—a Grenache, a Napa Gamay, a light Zinfandel or a young Petite Syrah. A hot, deep-flavored duck will take a rich red wine. However, in the notes to the following recipes, I will mention whites as well as reds for those who prefer them.

Chicken with Dill-Lemon Sauce   *Serves 6 to 8*

This is one of the first recipes I remember more or less devising for myself. It is equally good hot and aromatic or cold and jellied—either way it still gives me pleasure. Looking back, I see that one hallmark of my cooking—the extensive use of fresh lemon juice—had already sprung into being. Given that dill is now available in most parts of the country all year long, this is a recipe with the fresh taste of summer you can relish even in winter.

Lightly acid, chilled Sylvaner or White Riesling would be fresh and cool with this dish as long as it has no residual sugar. This makes for a light dinner or lunch accompanied by buttered noodles or a little rice. No vegetable is really needed; the green is provided by the ample dill.

4 tablespoons unsalted butter
2 2½-pound frying chickens, each
   cut into 8 serving pieces
1 large onion, chopped
   (approximately 1 cup)
¾ cup chopped dill
5 cups chicken stock (see Basic
   Recipes)
½ cup fresh lemon juice
1 tablespoon kosher salt
2 tablespoons cornstarch dissolved in
   2 tablespoons cold water

Melt the butter in a skillet. Add the chicken pieces in batches and cook just to sear them and eliminate the raw appearance, not to brown. As the pieces are done, put them in a stock pot.

Add the chopped onion and half the dill to the fat remaining in the pan and cook just until soft. Add to the chicken in the stock pot.

Deglaze the pan with some of the chicken stock, scraping well with a wooden spoon to incorporate all the cooking juices into the stock. Pour the contents of the pan and the rest of the chicken stock into the stock pot. Bring the liquid to a boil, then lower the heat to a simmer. Cook until the chicken is just tender, about 15 minutes.

Stir in the remaining dill, lemon juice and salt. The sauce should taste fresh and clear. Add some of the hot liquid to the cornstarch mixture; then stir that mixture into the stock pot. Raise the heat and cook just until the cornstarch dissolves and slightly thickens the sauce. The cornstarch leaves the sauce clear. If you cook it too long, however, the sauce will become thin again.

Chicken in Zinfandel

This dish is essentially a red fricassee whose ancestor is the French coq au vin. It demonstrates that even when the lesson from grand-père is quite literal, it still must be reworked for our American ingredients. First of all, unless one lives on a farm with free-range chickens, the chances are scant indeed of having a tough old cock around who will give up quantities of flavor on his way to becoming—over a long period of time—tender enough to eat. If we cook our defenseless young birds this way, they will become dry cardboard. The solution is to intensify the sauce without overly involving the bird. This can be done by a separate reduction of the broth and the judicious application of chicken glaze (see the Basic Recipes section). If you don't have any chicken glaze, you can do pretty well without. Do be careful to use a salt-free chicken stock. If you want to make the dish and only canned—and therefore salted—stock is available, omit salt from the recipe.

I add a little red wine vinegar at the end of the cooking because our wines are liable to be better and less acidic than the old gros rouge, *probably Algerian, that would have been used in this dish in France, and because a touch of red wine vinegar at the end can lighten the dish. Adding the garlic twice is not an affectation. Garlic that has been cooked a long time changes character and becomes sweet and slightly sticky, although aromatic. The garlic that is added toward the end of the cooking will zap up the sauce the way the vinegar does.*

The wine to drink is the wine you cook with: a clear, young Zinfandel—fragrant and red. Serve a steamed potato or some buttered noodles on the side. Follow with a green salad in French fashion that can be plopped on the chicken plate to blend in with the last bits of the wine sauce. Fruit, cheese and bread are about all you still need for such a full meal.

6 ounces bacon, cut in ¼-inch-thick slices
3-pound chicken, cut into serving pieces
¼ cup all-purpose flour
1 teaspoon kosher salt
Freshly ground black pepper
2 tablespoons California brandy
2 cups good Zinfandel
2 cups chicken stock (see Basic Recipes)
2 tablespoons tomato paste
1 bay leaf
¼ teaspoon dried thyme
8 medium-size cloves garlic
½ pound quartered mushrooms
½ pound small white onions

Cut the bacon into ½-by-1-inch pieces. Place them in a large skillet over medium heat. Cook until the pieces are crisp. Remove them with a slotted spoon and drain on absorbent paper, leaving the fat in the pan. If the bacon is very meaty and you have less than 2 tablespoons of fat in the pan, add a little oil. If you have more than 2 tablespoons of fat, pour off the extra.

Pat the chicken dry. Mix together the flour, salt and pepper on a plate. Coat each piece of chicken well with the flour, shaking off the excess, or put the chicken in a brown paper bag with the seasoned flour and shake well. Heat the fat in the pan and add the chicken pieces in a single layer, skin side down. Lightly brown the chicken; turn and brown the other side. Pour off the fat.

In a small pan, warm the brandy until you can see the blue glints. Ignite the brandy, pour it over the chicken, and let cook until the flames die down. Remove the chicken pieces

2 tablespoons unsalted butter

2 tablespoons chicken or meat glaze
 (see Basic Recipes, leave out if
 unavailable)

1½ teaspoons red wine vinegar, if
 necessary

to a plate and deglaze the pan with wine and stock. Stir in the tomato paste, bay leaf, thyme and 5 cloves garlic. Boil uncovered until reduced by half. Remove the bay leaf. Return the chicken to the skillet. Add the mushrooms. Reduce the heat and cover. Simmer about 20 to 30 minutes, or until the chicken is done.

Meanwhile, blanch the onions in the boiling water for a few minutes to loosen their skins. Peel and dry. Heat the butter in a skillet; add the onions and sauté until evenly brown and cooked through. Set aside.

Remove the chicken and mushrooms to a plate and keep warm. Skim the surface of the sauce of any grease. Raise the heat and stir in the chicken or meat glaze and the remaining 3 cloves garlic. Reduce the sauce to about 1½ cups, skimming the surface as it reduces.

Strain the sauce and taste. If necessary, add the vinegar, salt and pepper. Pour over the chicken and sprinkle with the reserved bacon and onions.

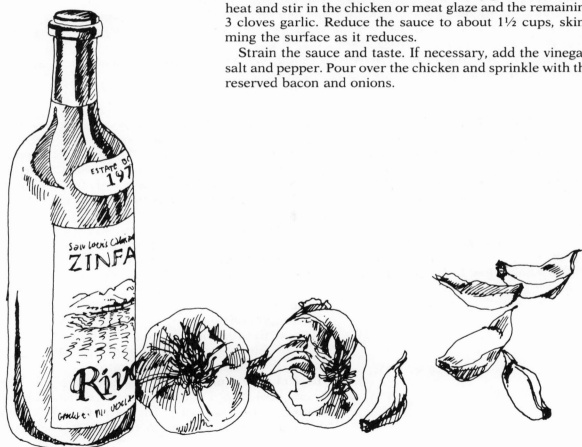

Duck Breasts with Rhubarb Sauce

Duck breasts, broiled as if they were steaks and then thinly sliced, are the current cliché of French cooking. Whole ducks are traditionally served with fruit sauces that cut and counterpoint the richness of the bird. The cherries of duck-with-cherries were meant to be bright red and tart, like our pie cherries. The oranges of duck-with-oranges were meant to be the rather bitter and acid red blood oranges. No sweetness was ever intended. This is my entry, from the American side, in the great duck sweepstakes: a duck breast with rhubarb—naturally acidic and brightly attractive. In the past, there was almost no farm or garden in America that did not contain at least a stand or two of rhubarb, and as it is the first fresh fruit of the spring, just before the sweet wild strawberries, it was mighty welcome.

The preparation technique for the duck is one I have adapted from André Daguin as brought to me by Paula Wolfert. The dry marination adds flavor, tenderizes and helps to remove some of the underskin fat. It does require that you think a day ahead and that you like your duck pink and juicy.

I hope you will like both the look and the taste of the dish's brown skin, creamy, pale-beige sauce and crisp, pink-red and grass-green vegetables.

A Blanc de Pinot Noir makes a marvelous complement to the flavor and hue of these duck breasts. The complexity of a Cabernet would also be pleasing.

Breasts from 4 5-pound ducks
8 cups diagonally sliced rhubarb
 (pieces should be 2 inches long)
4 cups diagonally sliced scallions
 (use both the green and white parts,
 cut into pieces about 1 inch long
 and very thin)
2 tablespoons kosher salt
1 teaspoon freshly ground black
 pepper
Rhubarb Sauce (see following recipe)

Begin this recipe the day before you plan to serve it.

You will need only the breasts from the ducks, boned. Cut each breast in half through the breast bone and remove all the bones, including the complete wings. Save them all for stock. Leave the skin on the breasts but trim off the excess skin and fat that hangs over and does not cover the meat.

Combine the rhubarb, scallions, salt and pepper. Place half in an 8-by-13-inch pan. Place the duck breasts in one layer over the mixture. Cover with the remaining rhubarb mixture. Cover the pan and refrigerate overnight.

Let the duck breasts reach room temperature before continuing.

Heat a grill or broiler.

Remove the duck breasts from the marinade and pat dry. Score the skin of each piece, cutting crosswise 4 or 5 times through the skin but not into the meat.

If you are broiling, place the breasts on a pan, skin side up, and cook 5 to 6 minutes; then turn and cook 1½ to 2 minutes on the flesh side. The meat should be pink and juicy. If grilling, the timings are the same, but begin with the breasts skin side down directly on the grill so that side cooks first.

Slice the breasts crosswise, holding your knife at a 45-degree angle to the cutting board. Serve with Rhubarb Sauce.

NOTE: Leftover legs and carcasses can go into your duck stock or the legs can be used to make the Duck Gumbo that you will find elsewhere in this book.

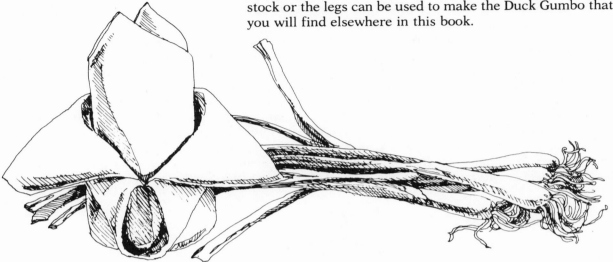

RHUBARB SAUCE

Makes about 3 cups

2 cups duck stock or chicken stock
5-6 tablespoons duck glaze or chicken glaze (see Basic Recipes)
¼ cup Cabernet Sauvignon or other red wine vinegar
1½ teaspoons kosher salt
Freshly ground black pepper
¾ pound unsalted butter, cut into 1-inch pieces
1⅓ cups diagonally sliced rhubarb (pieces should be ¾ inch long and very thin)
1 cup sliced scallions (use both the green and white parts, cut into pieces about ¼ inch long and very thin)
1 cup sliced radishes (pieces should be up to 1 inch long and very thin)

Pour the stock and glaze into a saucepan. Cook over medium heat until 1 cup remains. Add the vinegar, salt and a generous amount of pepper. Gradually beat in the butter piece by piece until the sauce is smooth. Stir in the rhubarb, scallions and radishes. Let sit off the heat before grilling the duck breasts. Before serving, taste for salt and pepper. Rhubarb tends to be salty.

Duck Gumbo

Gumbos, of course, are basic Cajun fare. A blending of French cooking and African and Spanish seasonings, they are perfect examples of integration and Americanization. Like much Louisiana food, they are thickened and enriched with a brown roux, which is simply equal quantities of butter and flour cooked long and slowly until the mixture reaches a rich, tawny color.

Almost any ingredient can serve as the base of a gumbo. I don't know if this one would qualify as authentic; although it is made with authentic ingredients, mine are not authentic hands.

Between the gelatinous stock, the brown roux, the okra and the filé, this gumbo turns into a very rich stew. Be careful not to overcook the okra and the filé or they will get stringy. The final seasoning will depend on the strength of your hot sauce—they dim with age—and your preference. Hot pepper sauces are often made with vinegar, but lemon seems to give them a fresher taste. The lemon at the end is also necessary to replace the acid that is drawn out of both tomatoes and peppers by prolonged cooking.

The acid is not so pronounced as to assault a wine. A good choice would be a Gewürztraminer, whose spiciness would complement that of the dish. I, however, prefer a red wine with duck. Try chilling a light Zinfandel or think of serving one of the daily-getting-better North Coast Pinot Noirs.

3 5-pound ducks
3 cups diced onion
¼ cup all-purpose flour
¼ cup minced garlic
7 tablespoons kosher salt
Freshly ground black pepper
2 teaspoons ground cayenne pepper
1½ teaspoons Tabasco sauce
2 35-ounce cans plum tomatoes
3 quarts duck stock made without
   salt (see Basic Recipes)
2 tablespoons lemon juice
5½ cups thinly sliced okra
2½ cups 3-inch-long julienned
   carrots
1½ cups shelled peas
4½ cups peeled asparagus spears,
   cut into 1-inch pieces
1 tablespoon filé powder
2 cups ¼-inch-thick diagonally
   sliced scallions (green and white
   parts)
Crystal Pure Louisiana hot sauce

GARNISH:
Thinly sliced scallions

Each duck needs to be cut into 16 pieces so that they are not unwieldy in the stew and will cook quickly. You will need a cleaver to cut through the bones, or a heavy knife and a hammer. Cut away any flapping pieces of skin and fat that are not covering the meat.

Heat a large casserole. Add a layer of duck pieces. Cook, turning as necessary, until the duck has lost its raw look and no traces of blood remain. Place the pieces in a sieve over a bowl to let the excess fat drain off. Continue cooking the duck pieces in the same way until they are all done. Pour off all but ¼ cup of the fat in the pan. Stir in the onions and let cook for a few minutes, or until they soften slightly. Add the flour and garlic, and cook for about 5 minutes, stirring constantly, until the mixture is brown. Do not let it burn. Stir in the salt, freshly ground black pepper, 1 teaspoon cayenne and 1 teaspoon Tabasco sauce. Cook for a minute.

Drain the tomatoes, then crush them with your hands and add to the casserole with the stock and 1 tablespoon lemon juice. Simmer the mixture for 30 minutes.

Add the duck and simmer for 15 minutes, skimming the fat constantly. Reserve some of the seasoned fat for the rice.

Add the okra and carrots and keep cooking and skimming until they are soft.

Stir in the peas and asparagus. When they are cooked through, stir in the filé powder and scallions. Cook until the mixture thickens slightly.

Adjust seasoning to taste, adding the remaining 1 teaspoon cayenne, ½ teaspoon Tabasco, 1 tablespoon lemon juice and a few drops of Louisiana hot sauce. The flavor should be spicy but not overwhelming.

Sprinkle some scallions over each portion. Serve with rice that has been cooked in a little less water than usual so that it is somewhat sticky, and seasoned with the reserved duck fat (2 to 3 tablespoons per pound of rice).

NOTE: If you have made the Duck Breasts with Rhubarb and have leftover duck legs, they can be used in this recipe. The legs and thighs of 2 ducks would replace 1 duck.

Raspberry-Glazed Roast Turkey with Duxelles Stuffing   *Serves 8*

There are all kinds of turkey stuffings, but I think this one is super de luxe. It puts turkey right back on the ten-most-festive list, especially when the skin is glazed with rosy raspberries.

The mushroom growers of Pennsylvania and California have put us all in their debt by making mushrooms regularly and inexpensively available. The profusion of mushrooms has made possible this stuffing, which is related to the classic French duxelles. The native pecans and the celery add crunch and flavor; onions, liver and seasonings do their bit as well.

When buying mushrooms, look for those that are smooth and light in color. This means they are fresh. Do, however, watch out for mushrooms that have been treated with citric acid or other preservatives. You can't tell how old they are, and they will have an "off" flavor.

You can serve this dish with the same wine that is used in the sauce, although for a special feast you may want to go up a notch in quality. You won't need a separate vegetable unless the occasion requires one. (You can use any leftover meat in a salad.)

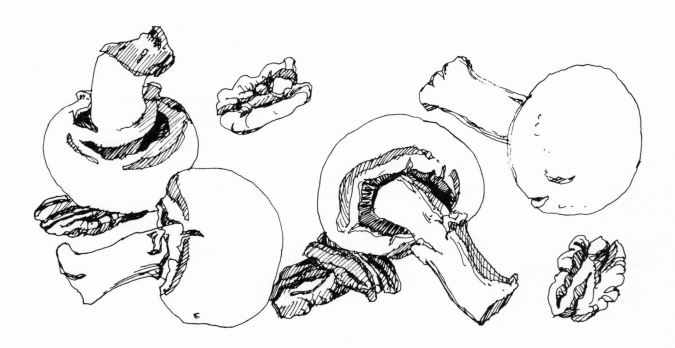

12-ounce jar raspberry jelly
Juice of 2 lemons
4 small cloves garlic, left whole
4½ pounds mushrooms, cleaned
10 ounces unsalted butter
2 packed cups coarsely chopped
 onions
8-pound turkey, liver reserved and
 cut into ¾-inch chunks
1½ cups coarsely chopped celery
1½ cups roughly chopped pecan
 pieces
2 tablespoons kosher salt
1 teaspoon celery seed
Freshly ground black pepper
¼ teaspoon Tabasco sauce
3 large eggs
½ cup Johannisberg Riesling
 or Cabernet Sauvignon

Put the jelly, lemon juice and garlic in a saucepan and cook over medium heat until reduced to half. This is the glaze.

Heat the oven to 500 degrees.

In batches, chop the mushrooms in a food processor until they are in tiny pieces. Do not overprocess them so that they turn to mush.

Melt ½ pound butter in a wide (12- to 14-inch) deep pan over medium heat. Add the mushrooms and turn them in the butter until they have all changed color. Raise the heat and let boil rapidly until the mixture is almost completely dry.

While the mushrooms cook, heat the remaining 4 tablespoons butter in a separate skillet. Add the chopped onions and cook for a few minutes, or until they are translucent.

When the mushrooms are dry, turn off the heat. Add the onions, liver, celery, pecans, salt, celery seed, pepper and Tabasco. Mix well.

Stuff about two-thirds of the mixture into the turkey, working from both ends. Pull the neck flap over the stuffing and secure in place with a skewer.

Place the turkey in a roasting pan, breast side up. Roast in the preheated oven for 30 minutes.

Mix the remaining third of the stuffing with the eggs. Place in a ceramic ovenproof dish.

After the turkey has roasted for 30 minutes, brush it generously with the glaze. Put the extra stuffing in the oven. Continue roasting the turkey for another 30 minutes, basting every 10 minutes with the glaze.

The turkey should be done after an hour's roasting time.

Place the turkey on a platter and remove the stuffing from the cavity.

Pour any fat (there shouldn't be much) out of the roasting pan. Place the pan over high heat. Pour in the wine and scrape the bottom to deglaze the caramelized bits. Serve this as your gravy.

Serve with the 2 stuffings on the side.

Turkey Salad with Buttermilk Dressing

Serves 4

The day after turkey means leftovers. While turkey hash is good, another bout of real cooking may seem too much. With this recipe you have an ample salad that is fresh and quite different from hot turkey. At lunch it might serve as many as six. As fresh as the salad would be a well-chilled rosé wine.

The salad dressing is worth remembering for other occasions. It is not only light-tasting but light in calories as well.

2 tablespoons unsalted butter
1 cup mushrooms (whole if small, quartered if large)
1 large green bell pepper, cut into ¾-inch squares
2 cups cooked turkey, skinned, boned and cut into ¾-inch cubes
2 10-ounce baking potatoes, baked, still warm, peeled and cut into ¾-inch chunks
¼ packed cup coarsely chopped fresh coriander
½ cup scallions, green and white parts cut into ¼-inch-thick rounds

DRESSING:
½ cup buttermilk
2 tablespoons cider vinegar
¼ cup olive oil
½ teaspoon kosher salt
Freshly ground black pepper
3 drops Tabasco sauce
¼ teaspoon celery seed
⅛ teaspoon Worcestershire sauce

GARNISH:
1 head of chicory
Cucumber slices
Tomato slices
Whole coriander leaves

Heat the butter in an 8-inch skillet over medium heat. Add the mushrooms and toss to coat. Cook for about 30 seconds. Add the green pepper, stir to combine and cook for about 3 minutes, or until the mushrooms begin to brown.

Meanwhile mix the turkey, potatoes, coriander and scallions in a large bowl. Add the mushroom-and-pepper mixture and toss.

To prepare the dressing combine the buttermilk, vinegar, oil, salt, black pepper, Tabasco sauce, celery seed and Worcestershire sauce. Pour the dressing over the ingredients in the bowl. Toss to blend all the ingredients and to coat everything with the dressing.

To serve, arrange some chicory on one side of 4 large plates and overlap cucumber and tomato slices on the other side. Put some of the salad in the center of each plate and top with some of the coriander leaves.

SEAFOOD & FISH

When the English-speaking explorers came to this country, they found a land of plenty where fish teemed in the shallow ocean waters and in the rivers. We have depleted that plenty, but much yet remains. Fish that is fresh should be cooked simply.

One of our royal ingredients is Maine lobster. Some people broil, some people bake, some people sauce; I don't. To me lobster is at its best briefly boiled in seawater. Since I prefer body meat to claw meat, I often buy culls—those victims of frequent battles of the deep with only one claw left. They are significantly less expensive. Although I have tasted primordial monsters that were tender and sweet, I favor small lobsters, 1 to 1½ pounds. They should be cooked no more than 10 to 12 minutes. French cookbooks will always lead you astray—their lobsters or saltwater crawfish seem to need extended cooking that would turn an American lobster leathery. Some melted butter and a half lemon, already messy clothes and good will are all the additions required.

Striped bass and speckled trout are among our better fish that should be simply poached. Boil enough water to cover the fish. Season it if you wish: an inexpensive, cleanly made white wine, some cloves of garlic, some pepper and a bay leaf. Reduce the water temperature to a simmer and cook 10 minutes for each inch or fraction of an inch of thickness of the fish. Pan broiling in a heavy iron skillet isn't bad for small fish.

Scallops of all sizes are at their best raw or as close to it as you can manage by sautéing or broiling. Raw is also best for clams and oysters.

If you live near the shore, you may feel some need for variation. Of the flounder family, only the nonresident Dover sole is so splendid that it requires no embellishment beyond a brief poaching or sautéing. Some fish, such as shad, are too fragile for poaching.

Clams and oysters have always been the occasion for the driest of chilled white wines: a perfectly dry Sauvignon Blanc or a Johannisberg Riesling made without any residual sugar in the French rather than the German style, a Chenin Blanc from flinty soil such as Monterey, or even a Chardonnay from a producer who doesn't like too much oak or too heavy a wine. A dry sparkling wine is another classic accompaniment.

When we get to lobster, with its heavy perfume, these wines will still do, but a full, rich Chardonnay or a Johannisberg Riesling with a hint of sweetness will rise to greater heights.

Cream sauces and fattier fish can also take the richer wines, but fried fish and seafood will be happier with a light wine that has a touch of acidity.

If you have a white table or jug wine that you like, chill it well and serve it amply. Better to spend less money and have more wine, especially at party times such as a clambake or an outdoor lobster boil.

Shrimp Étouffé   *Serves 4*

Here we are on the treacherous ground of regional food, where each person and no person is an expert. "Étouffé" tells us we are in the Louisiana of the French settlers. The hot peppers tell us there has been contact with lands that used to be called South of the Border. The cooking style tells us of black cooks with African roots. The Worcestershire sauce seems to be authentic, strangely enough. The wine and the shrimp butter are pure me.

In Louisiana, several kinds of fresh shrimp abound, and, in season, mud bugs or crawfish are used for this dish. Those of us who do not live in such a favored area will all be using frozen shrimp. When you see shrimp in a market that are not frozen and are lying singly on ice, this means that they have been defrosted. You are better off buying the shrimp frozen and defrosting them as you need them. When I have a block of frozen shrimp that is larger than I need, I pick up the whole block, unwrapped but still frozen, and bring it down with a whack on the edge of a counter, causing the block to sunder. I defrost what I need and go on from there.

Traditionally, this is a spicy dish, although the degree of spiciness is up to you. An elegant or restrained wine would be wasted here. A fruity Chenin Blanc or a good-quality white table wine is a delight.

The only tricky part of the preparation is making the brown roux basic to many New Orleans dishes. Don't rush the browning of the flour in the butter; it takes time. When the roux is a good color, remove it from the heat and stir. What you don't want is for the flour to scorch.

**4 tablespoons Shrimp Butter
(see following recipe)**
¼ cup all-purpose flour
1 cup finely chopped onions
½ cup finely chopped celery
1 teaspoon finely chopped garlic
**1 cup peeled and seeded chopped
tomatoes**
1½ cups dry white wine
1 tablespoon Worcestershire sauce
1½ teaspoons kosher salt
**½ teaspoon freshly ground black
pepper**
½ teaspoon Tabasco sauce
**1 pound shrimp, shells removed,
tails left on**
½ cup chopped scallions
2 teaspoons fresh lemon juice

Melt the shrimp butter in a non-aluminum skillet and stir in the flour. Cook over low heat, stirring frequently, until the mixture turns a nutty dark brown. Stir in the onions, celery and garlic. Cook, stirring often, until the onions and celery are softened, about 10 minutes longer.

Stir in the tomatoes and wine and cook another 3 to 5 minutes. Stir in the Worcestershire sauce, salt, pepper and Tabasco with the shrimp and scallions. Cover and cook for 3 to 5 minutes, or until the shrimp are just barely cooked. Season with lemon juice.

Serve over hot rice.

SHRIMP BUTTER

Raw shells from 1 pound shrimp
½ pound unsalted butter

Makes about 1 cup

Rinse the shrimp shells and any unused bits of shrimp in water. Dry well. Melt the butter over medium heat in a heavy-bottomed non-aluminum pot. When the butter has melted, add the shrimp shells; cook, stirring constantly, for 10 minutes.

Put the shells and butter into a food processor and process for 2 minutes. Return the shells and butter to the pot. Cook over gentle heat for 15 minutes. Strain the mixture through a very fine sieve, pushing with a wooden spoon to extract all the butter possible. The mixture will now be a lovely pale-pink mass.

Refrigerated, the butter will keep for a week; frozen, indefinitely. A teaspoonful or so of this butter can enrich innumerable fish and seafood sauces.

Seafood Succotash

Succotash is the New England version of the all-in-one-pot stew. Winter succotashes were made with dried corn and dried lima beans. Summer succotashes were made with fresh kernels scraped off the cob and tiny, sweet lima beans. I thought it would be fun to make a sort of nouvelle-cuisine succotash using the great New England lobster and seafoods. The result is a smashing combination of colors, textures and flavors. If you feel the need for a first course, Watercress Mousse with Raw Ham (in the First Courses section) would be a good idea. Finish with fresh fruit or the lightest possible fruit sorbet. Such a meal would permit you a crisp Sauvignon Blanc or Chenin Blanc throughout.

1½-pound live lobster
1 tablespoon unsalted butter
1 tablespoon olive oil
½ teaspoon minced garlic
12 large shrimp, peeled, tails left on
2 tablespoons bourbon
4 cups peeled, seeded, roughly chopped tomatoes
½ cup chopped parsley
1½-2 teaspoons kosher salt
Generous amount of freshly ground black pepper
Pinch cayenne pepper
18 mussels, well scrubbed and debearded
Lima Bean and Corn Mixture (see following recipe)

Cut the lobster into 16 pieces as follows:

Place the lobster on its stomach, holding it securely against your work surface. With a cook's knife, cut the tail from the body in a single hard, downward motion. If your knife isn't heavy enough, tap it firmly with a hammer.

Next, cut the tail in half lengthwise. Cut each half crosswise into 4 pieces. Set aside.

Grasp the body firmly in one hand and grasp a claw securely in the other hand. Twist and pull off the claw. Repeat with the other claw. Cut off the very end of the claw, if necessary—it won't always come away with the claw. Break the claw at the joint into two pieces. Remove the plug or band holding the claw together; then cut each claw in half crosswise.

Finally, place the lobster body on the work surface, bottom up. Place a cook's knife in position to split the lobster in half lengthwise. Using a hammer, tap on the top of the knife to cut the lobster evenly in half. Remove and discard the stomach and the small yellow sac.

Heat the butter and oil in a large skillet. When hot, add the garlic, lobster and shrimp. Cook, stirring or shaking often, for about 1 minute. Pour on the bourbon and ignite.

When the flames die down, remove the shellfish to a plate. Add the tomatoes, parsley, salt and peppers to the pan. Cover and cook over high heat about 3 minutes, or until the tomatoes begin to give off liquid.

Add the mussels, lobster and shrimp with any liquid that has accumulated on the plate. Cover the pan and cook 2 minutes, shaking the pan occasionally, until the mussels have opened.

Taste the sauce and season with more salt and pepper if necessary.

To serve, spoon some Lima Bean and Corn Mixture in a ring on each plate. Spoon the seafood mixture into the center.

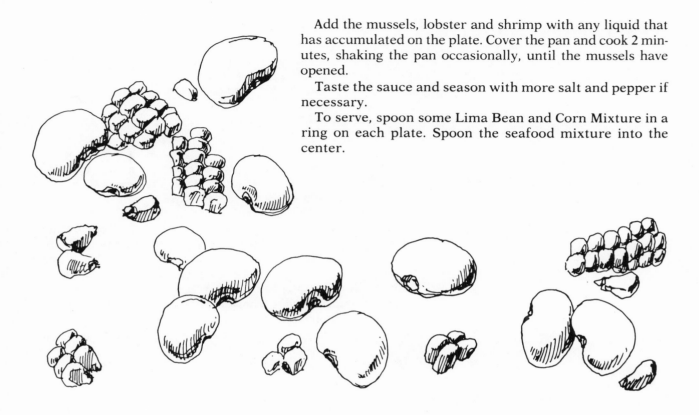

LIMA BEAN AND CORN MIXTURE

6 ears fresh corn
3 tablespoons unsalted butter
1½ teaspoons minced garlic
6 10-ounce packages frozen baby lima beans, thawed and drained
3 cups heavy cream
6 tablespoons chopped fresh chives
2¼ teaspoons kosher salt
Freshly ground black pepper
4½ tablespoons fresh lemon juice

Using a sharp knife, scrape all the kernels off the corn cobs into a bowl. Set aside. Discard the cobs.

Heat the butter in a large skillet and add the garlic. Cook over moderate heat for about 30 seconds. Add the lima beans, corn and cream. Simmer over low heat for about 10 minutes. Stir in the chives, then season with salt, pepper and lemon juice.

You can serve immediately or let the flavors mellow overnight in the refrigerator. Reheat before serving. If the mixture is too thick, add a little more cream.

Shad Fillets in Butter

Serves 6 to 8

Everybody seems to welcome shad roe, but too often the shad itself is relegated to a secondary position. I think shad is a fabulous fish in its own right, but you must get it from somebody who really knows how to bone it, because shad is filled with a myriad of tiny bones. Boned shad cooks quickly and is meltingly good.

I like to serve a full-bodied Chardonnay or a full-bodied but not sweet table wine.

½ cup plus 3 tablespoons melted unsalted butter

2 1-pound fillets of whole, headless shad

Heat the broiler.

You will need a shallow baking dish large enough to allow the fillets to fit in a single layer. Pour 3 tablespoons butter into the dish and spread it to cover the bottom.

Arrange the fillets, skin side down, in the dish. Open up the flaps of the fish and pour in ¼ cup butter, evenly distributing it between the fillets. Pour the remaining ¼ cup butter evenly over the fish.

Set the fish aside at room temperature for about 15 minutes, or until the butter solidifies.

Broil about 3 inches from the heat source for 15 minutes. Turn off the heat and leave in the oven for another 5 minutes, or until the fish is opaque when you look under a flap.

Serve hot.

MEAT

If we are indeed a meat-and-potatoes nation, then the vegetarians and the increasing number of fish eaters and the endless miles of chicken sold are all a mistake. Nevertheless, from a wine drinker's point of view, meat and cheese belong in menus to set off the fullest, richest and most elegant of red wines. It is in this category that we find the Cabernets, the Merlots, the Pinot Noirs and some of the Zinfandels. Just as we as a nation have changed from non-wine drinkers to pop-wine drinkers to white-wine drinkers, I think we will eventually become red-wine drinkers. While I will drink red wine with almost anything, and so will many of my vegetarian friends, the undisputed buddy of red wine—other than cheese—is meat.

Beef and Scallop Sauté

It occurred to me one day that while the Chinese and Japanese had their soys and the Filipinos, Indonesians and Vietnamese their anchovy sauces, we had developed no salty liquid to dash into recipes when a bit of immediate seasoning was required, and so I made the flavored brine used in this recipe. It can be kept in the refrigerator practically forever.

The colors of the beef and scallops together are particularly attractive. Strangely enough, it is the beef that picks up the delicate flavor of the scallops rather than the scallops being overwhelmed by the flavor of the beef. It is an elegant dish. I don't think it requires rice or another starch served with it; some bread, or better yet a spoon, would be the best way to get up the last of the sauce. Serve a Zinfandel made in the French style.

2 tablespoons peanut oil
1 teaspoon minced garlic
1 pound trimmed beef tenderloin,
    cut crosswise into ½-inch-thick
    pieces, then halved
¾ pound sea scallops
1¼ cups diagonally sliced scallions,
    (white and green parts)
1 tablespoon Flavored Salt Brine
    (see following recipe)
Freshly ground black pepper
Pinch red pepper flakes

Heat the oil in a wok or large skillet until very hot, almost smoking. Add the garlic and beef, then the scallops. Cook, stirring, for about 30 seconds. Add the scallions, brine, pepper and pepper flakes. Cook for another 30 seconds.

FLAVORED SALT BRINE

Makes about 1½ cups

2 cups water
2 tablespoons sliced, peeled fresh
    ginger
1 tablespoon freshly ground white
    pepper
1 teaspoon dried red pepper flakes
1½ cups kosher salt

Put the water, ginger, white pepper and pepper flakes in a saucepan and bring to a boil. Gradually stir in the salt. Reduce the heat and simmer for 10 minutes. Strain the mixture through a sieve lined with a damp kitchen towel. Keep in a covered jar in the refrigerator.

Steak with Green Peppercorn-Bourbon Sauce

Serves 6

Pepper steaks have become a favorite steakhouse item. This version, with brine-packed green peppercorns from Madagascar, Kentucky bourbon and French wine vinegar, has a slightly different American lilt. Any good Cabernet, Pinot Noir, Merlot or Zinfandel would go well with it.

6 tablespoons vegetable oil
¾ cup chopped shallots
6 garlic cloves, mashed
¾ cup bourbon
6 cups chicken stock (see Basic
    Recipes)
¾ cup meat glaze (see Basic Recipes)
6 tablespoons brine-packed green
    peppercorns, drained and mashed
Kosher salt
1-2 tablespoons red wine vinegar
4-pound steak

Heat a grill or broiler until very hot.

Heat the oil in a skillet. Add the shallots and garlic and cook, stirring, until they are soft.

Heat the bourbon in a small pan. Light it with a match; then pour it, still flaming, into the skillet. Shake the pan until the flames die down.

Discard the garlic. Stir in the stock and cook until reduced to half.

Add the glaze and green peppercorns. Continue cooking until the sauce is reduced to about 2 cups. Season to taste with salt and vinegar. Keep warm until the steak is ready.

Grill or broil the steak to the desired degree of doneness. Let it rest for a few minutes, then slice and serve with the sauce.

Roast Loin of Pork with Spicy Pears

Serves 4 to 6

Today's pork is much less fatty than it used to be. We also know that pork does not have to be cooked to death to make it safe to eat. I like pork roasted, with or without the pear sauce. Cold roast pork is wonderful, and I often make extra just to have leftovers. The sauce may seem a bit strange at first, but spiced pears have been a classic on Pennsylvania Dutch tables for centuries.

This roast goes well with a white wine—a Chardonnay or a dry Johannisberg Riesling. My choice would be a well-made Napa Zinfandel.

6-inch loin of pork (approximately 3 pounds), boned and rolled, bones reserved
2 medium-size cloves garlic, cut into slivers
1 tablespoon fresh rosemary or 1 teaspoon dried rosemary
Kosher salt
Freshly ground black pepper
2 tablespoons unsalted butter
¼ teaspoon minced garlic
4 cups peeled, cored, sliced pears (about 4 pears, each cut into 12 wedges)
¼ cup dry red wine
3 tablespoons red currant jelly
2 tablespoons soy sauce
2 teaspoons red wine vinegar
Cayenne pepper

Heat the oven to 500 degrees.

With a pointed knife, make slits in an even pattern in the fat side of the pork. Insert the garlic into the slits. Turn the pork over and insert a few slivers of garlic where the meat overlaps. Pat the skin all over, including the ends, with the rosemary, salt and black pepper.

Place the bones in a roasting pan so they stand up like a rack. Place the pork on them and roast the meat for 45 minutes in the preheated oven, or until the internal temperature of the pork reaches 140 degrees.

Heat the butter in a skillet. Add the minced garlic and pears. Cover and cook over medium-high heat until the pears are almost tender, about 2 to 5 minutes. Remove the pears with a slotted spoon and set aside until the pork has finished cooking. Remove the skillet from the heat.

Remove the pork and bones from the roasting pan and pour off the fat. Place the pan over heat and stir in the wine, scraping the bottom to deglaze the pan. Add about 3 tablespoons of this liquid to the skillet in which the pears cooked, along with the currant jelly, soy sauce and vinegar. Mix well and cook until about ¼ cup liquid remains.

Return the pears to the skillet and cook briefly to reheat them, tossing so that they are coated with the sauce. Season to taste with salt and cayenne pepper. Slice the pork and serve with the spicy pears.

If you wish, cut up the pork bones and place them under the broiler until brown and crisp on all sides. Serve as an extra treat on the side.

Pork Salad with Soy Dressing

If you, by chance or intent, have leftover roast pork, use it in this wonderful salad enriched by borrowings from the Chinese grocer. Fortunately for all of us, these ingredients have become staples of the American kitchen as well.

    A smoky Fumé Blanc version of a Sauvignon Blanc would fit right in with these flavorings.

3½ tablespoons tarragon vinegar
3½ tablespoons Japanese soy sauce
¼ teaspoon dry mustard
Kosher salt
Freshly ground black pepper
½ teaspoon chopped, tightly packed
   fresh tarragon leaves, if available
6 tablespoons olive oil
Scant ¼ teaspoon Oriental sesame oil
4 cups leftover Roast Loin of Pork,
   cut into 2-by-½-by-¼-inch strips
   (see previous recipe)
4 cups sliced Chinese cabbage, cut on
   the diagonal, ¼-inch thick
1 cup mung bean sprouts
2 teaspoons finely chopped fresh
   ginger
2 teaspoons finely chopped garlic

Place the vinegar, soy, dry mustard, salt and pepper in a small bowl. Whisk to mix, then stir in the tarragon. Whisk in the olive and sesame oils until the mixture is blended.

Place the remaining ingredients in a serving bowl. Add the dressing and toss to mix well. Taste and adjust the seasonings as necessary.

Serve at room temperature.

Country-Smoked Ham Braised with Chardonnay

Serves up to 20

A good country ham smoked over a sweet wood such as apple or equally sweet smoldering corncobs is one of the great pleasures of American cooking. While it is festive, it is not prohibitively expensive. For Europeans a whole ham is a once-a-year rarity at New Year's or some other special occasion. European ham is normally thinly shaved and doled out in hors d'oeuvres.

Once we Americans serve the splendid beast, however, it is difficult to find a wine to have with it because it has a certain intrinsic sweetness as well as a voluptuous richness. We tend to reinforce this sweetness by the way we glaze our hams. It was not until a friend served me one of the large, full Napa Valley Chardonnays with an almost golden edge to the color that I finally found the perfect accompaniment for a good ham. The fullness and warmth, when coupled with the traditional oak, create the ideal partner for the rosy glow of ham.

A well-smoked ham does not require cooking but rather infusing with flavor and heating. I have taken a tip from the French by cooking the ham in liquid rather than roasting it dry. The poaching adds moisture to the ham, and the final oven braising adds flavor—from the Chardonnay mixed with a hint of richness from the port—and glazes.

To go with the ham, I suggest a dish that has both tradition and novelty—Grits Timbale (recipe follows in section on Side Dishes).

Whole smoked ham, untrimmed (size doesn't matter and will depend on the number of guests)

1 bottle (about 3 cups) California Chardonnay

½ cup California Tawny Port

½ cup sugar

Place the ham in a large pot. Pour in enough cold water to cover it. Bring the water to a boil. Immediately lower the heat so the water simmers, and let simmer for 1 hour.

Heat the oven to 300 degrees.

Remove the ham from the pot and place in a roasting pan. Pour the Chardonnay and port over the top of the ham. Cover the pan with aluminum foil and place in the lower third of the oven for 45 minutes.

Remove the pan from the oven and turn the oven to broil. (If using a gas oven, turn the heat up to the maximum temperature.)

Cut away the skin from the top of the ham. Score the fat in an attractive pattern. Pat the sugar into the fat in an even layer. (If the top seems dry, sprinkle some of the cooking liquid over it.)

Return the ham to the oven until it begins to brown and form a nice crust. Keep it on the low shelf away from the broiler so it browns without burning.

Transfer the ham to a platter.

Pour the pan juices into a saucepan. Bring to a boil and skim off the fat. Pour into a gravy boat.

To serve, carve the ham as you would a leg of lamb, slicing down the bone against the grain. Place a slice of ham on each plate with an unmolded Grits Timbale. Spoon some gravy over the ham and serve with some herbal or spicy mustard on the side. If you feel the plate needs color, add a sprig of watercress.

Lamb Medallions with Mint and Tomatoes

Serves 4 to 6

Beef is not the only thing that has a steak. A nice and unexpected way to serve lamb is in medallions. The seasoning of this dish owes something to the Greeks; the procedure is pure American, in a hurry; the result is home or party fare.

I choose the wine inversely by quality to the number of guests. Four people will take the wine seriously: a fine, vintage Cabernet. Twelve guests will barely notice what they are drinking: an unassuming Zinfandel. If it is just for me and mine, it depends how I am feeling about everybody that day.

2 racks of lamb, or 8 2-inch-round,
   1-inch-thick boneless medallions
   of lamb plus 1 to 1½ pounds lamb
   bones
4 tablespoons unsalted butter
2 teaspoons finely chopped garlic
2 tablespoons finely chopped shallots
1 scant cup peeled, seeded, coarsely
   chopped tomatoes
14 fresh mint leaves
2 tablespoons fresh lemon juice
Freshly ground black pepper
2 teaspoons kosher salt

If using the racks of lamb, cut the center "eyes" from the bones so you have 2 long, round pieces of lamb. Cut each crosswise into 4 even pieces, each about 1 inch thick. Trim the fat from the meat and bones and discard. Place the bones and any meat trimmings in a pot.

If using boneless medallions, use the extra bones. Either way, cover the bones with cold water and simmer for 1 hour, skimming as needed. Strain the stock and reduce to about half.

Melt the butter in an 8- to 9-inch skillet over medium heat. Add the garlic and shallots and sauté for 30 seconds. Place the lamb medallions in the pan in a single layer and cook until lightly brown on both sides.

Add the tomatoes and cook for 1 to 2 minutes. Add the mint leaves and cook for another minute. Add the lemon juice, pepper, salt and ½ cup of the lamb stock. Cook for 2 to 3 minutes longer.

Serve with fresh noodles.

NOTE: This is an easy recipe to increase. If you do make larger quantities, be sure to use a larger skillet so you can cook all the meat at once.

SIDE DISHES

We are growing more and more vegetables and growing them well. When I go to the store, in addition to native American corn, tomatoes, potatoes, peppers, beans and squashes, I also find European, Chinese, Japanese, Mexican, Thai, South American and Near Eastern vegetables and fruits. I can choose to make a wide variety of traditional vegetables and side dishes, such as Seafood Succotash (in the Seafood section), or numerous pickles and farm jellies and quick breads. In this chapter, I just want to indicate a few new ways to think about traditional subjects.

Grits Timbale   *Serves 6*

Grits is (although I am from New York, I have had the lesson pounded in: in the South, grits take the singular verb) an especially American food. Before the discovery of the Americas, Europeans had no corn.

To make hominy, the corn is subjected to a sophisticated process. First, it is soaked in lye to swell the kernels and pop their skins. It is then washed to remove all traces of lye, drained and dried, then finally ground to turn it into grits.

With this ubiquitous Southern food, we have made a very sophisticated little side dish—creamy as breakfast grits, elegant as a three-star meal, with just a touch of garlic to keep it from being too refined.

For ramekins you can use actual French metal timbales, brown ceramic American custard cups, or small soufflé dishes. Just be sure to put the same amount into each dish, or the cooking time will vary.

This can be served with Country-Smoked Ham Braised with Chardonnay (in the Meat section) or any sautéed dish, sauced or not. Once you get the hang of it, it's an easy, posh and versatile dish.

4 cups water
2¼ teaspoons kosher salt
1 cup grits (not quick-cooking)
⅛ teaspoon mashed, minced garlic
¼ pound unsalted butter, cut into pieces
4 large eggs, lightly beaten
3 large egg yolks
Freshly ground black pepper
Pinch cayenne pepper

Heat the oven to 350 degrees. Grease 6 6-ounce ramekins and set aside.

Bring the water and 1½ teaspoons salt to a boil in a saucepan. Stir in the grits. Cook for 25 to 30 minutes, stirring frequently to keep the mixture from sticking. Stir in the garlic and butter. Remove from the heat.

Beat the eggs, egg yolks, ¾ teaspoon salt and peppers together in a bowl, just to mix. Stir quickly into the hot grits. Pour into the prepared ramekins. Cover each with buttered foil, buttered side down. Place them in a baking dish and add hot water to the dish to come halfway up the sides of the ramekins.

Bake for 30 minutes.

Unmold onto a plate to serve.

Pepper Pear Bread

Makes 2 ring loaves

This rye, pear and pepper-flavored bread is extremely attractive to look at. I don't serve it with an elegant meal, but with cheese or a light salad it is an unexpected treat. It also toasts well.

2 medium-size pears
½ cup water
½ teaspoon freshly ground black pepper
¼-ounce package dry yeast
2 tablespoons honey
2 teaspoons kosher salt
3 large eggs
1 cup rye flour
3 to 4 cups all-purpose flour
1 tablespoon milk

Peel and core the pears. Cut them into small pieces. Steam over ½ cup simmering water until fork-tender. Remove the pears and reduce the water to 1 tablespoon. Puree the pears with the reduced water and the pepper in a food processor.

Pour the pear puree into the bowl of an electric mixer and mix with the yeast, honey, salt and 2 eggs.

Add the rye flour and 1 cup all-purpose flour. Slowly knead until incorporated. Slowly add 2 more cups all-purpose flour. If necessary, slowly add a little more flour until the mixture cleans the side of the bowl. If it feels sticky, add flour, 1 tablespoon at a time, until the dough becomes smooth and soft to the touch.

Remove the bowl from the mixer and cover it tightly with plastic wrap. Let it sit at room temperature for about

1 hour, or until the dough doubles in volume. If the dough does not bounce back when poked with a finger, it is ready.

Remove the plastic covering and knead the dough for 30 seconds to expel the air bubbles. Divide the dough into 2 pieces and form each into a ball. Flatten 1 ball by pressing down, then pierce its center with 2 fingers. Slowly work this into a large hole by carefully pulling against the sides of the hole with both hands as the dough rests on the table. Let the dough rotate as your hands gradually enlarge the hole to 3 inches. Turn the dough over and pinch the dough together along the circle in order to firm up the shape. Turn it over again and place on a baking sheet. Repeat with the second half.

Let the shaped dough rise for about 45 minutes or until doubled.

About 20 minutes before the dough is ready to bake, heat the oven to 350 degrees. Make a glaze with the remaining egg and the milk and brush it over the raised bread. If you wish, sprinkle with freshly ground black pepper.

Bake for 30 to 40 minutes, or until the top and bottom are nicely browned and the bread sounds hollow when tapped.

Cool the bread on a cooling rack.

Zucchini Custard

This is a sort of crustless quiche or a not very high-rising soufflé. Cooked in individual portions, it makes a nice, light first course. As a single offering, it is marvelous with any simply prepared meat: grilled fish, roast chicken, leg of lamb or roast loin of pork. For vegetarians, this dish offers a perfect nutritional whole. For the Americanophiles among us, it illustrates this book's point: American green squash—whatever we have learned to call it—French technique and Italian cheese combine into a creamy American whole.

The only trick is to drain the zucchini well so that the custard does not get watery. You don't need any salt because the Parmesan has plenty. I have an old Bennington custard baking dish that I use for this custard. The mottled, rich brown sets off the creamy white custard beautifully. When this is baked, there is a surprising continuity between custard and zucchini. If the surprise element doesn't interest you, leave on the skins, as long as they have not been waxed; the green strips will give color contrast. The easiest way to mix the ingredients together is the most basic—with your hands.

2 pounds small, firm zucchini, peeled and cut into 2-inch-long, ¼-inch-square strips
1½ cups heavy cream
3 large eggs
½ to ¾ cup freshly grated Parmesan cheese
Freshly ground black pepper

Bring about 6 quarts of heavily salted water to a boil. Add the zucchini and let the water return to the boil. Boil for 30 seconds, then drain. Spread the zucchini in a single layer on kitchen towels and let dry for several hours, or all day.

Heat the oven to 450 degrees.

Mix the zucchini with the cream, eggs, cheese and pepper. Pour the mixture into a 9- or 10-inch pie plate or ceramic quiche pan.

Place on a baking sheet in the lower third of the preheated oven and bake for 40 minutes, or until puffed, brown, custardy and set.

Serve immediately.

NOTE: If you prefer individual servings, divide the mixture among 8 6-ounce ceramic quiche pans and bake only 15 to 20 minutes.

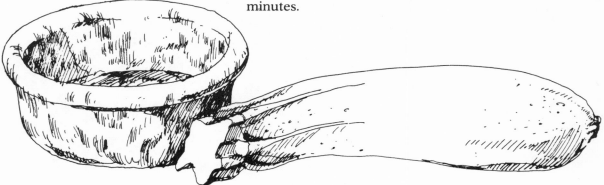

DESSERTS

I said earlier that we were in the middle of an American culinary revolution, defining an American style. When it comes to desserts, this country has already had one revolution. American-invented baking powder and an abundance of pure white flour—once available only to the wealthy in large parts of Europe—provoked a flurry of baking and invention. The discovery of cornmeal was the impetus for many new desserts. The independence and isolation of farms from villages required housewives to make for themselves many things which in Europe would have been bought from the village baker.

Out from the farm wives' ovens rolled biscuits and breads and layer cakes, angel food cakes and devil's food cakes, coconut cakes and apple pies. Most households had their own chickens and eggs, and there were incredibly good chiffon pies and custard pies. All these recipes exist in many excellent books, and I see no need to reinvent them.

I must confess that I am not much of a dessert eater; like an Italian, I am usually happy with fruit and cheese at the end of a meal. Fresh berries with cream; or with raspberry vinegar, sugar and black pepper; or with lemon juice and sugar are for me a sufficient summer dissipation. But I have guests, and they like dessert.

Sometimes what I do is as simple as hollowing out a ripe papaya, filling the hollow with sour cream and patting a layer of brown sugar over the cream. Left to sit for a half hour, the acid in the cream caramelizes the sugar—and we have a delight to eat with a spoon. Sometimes I poach peaches in a fragrant syrup, peel them and surround them with fresh raspberries, which I then lightly bathe with a reduction of the poaching syrup. Whipped cream would be an almost sinful extra.

Occasionally a real dessert is required. Here are a few of my living-up-to-the-occasion desserts.

We tend not to have the habit of dessert wine in America. Sometimes a little Champagne will be left from the beginning of a festive meal, and it will be served with dessert, but rarely is wine deliberately served. This is a shame, since California is beginning to produce some excellent dessert wines. As a non-dessert person I am often delighted to have a glass or more of a Selected Late Harvest or other botrytized or sugar-rich wine instead of dessert. The best of these wines tend to be expensive but small quantities are usually sufficient. A good Johannisberg Riesling that has a fair amount of residual sugar will generally be less costly. I find that a dessert wine always adds a festive note, and in a meal where there is just a main course and a dessert it gives the opportunity for two wines and two sparkling glasses.

Sweet Tomato Tart   *Serves 12*

This tart is a bit of a surprise. Both in classes and at the table it has proved successful—pretty, too.

2 cups all-purpose flour
7 tablespoons unsalted butter, cut into ½-inch slices
Pinch kosher salt
6 tablespoons ice water (approximately)
1 egg mixed with 1 teaspoon water
2 tablespoons blanched julienned orange zest
2 tablespoons blanched julienned lemon zest
2 tablespoons brown sugar
4 ripe beefsteak tomatoes, thinly sliced, drained and patted dry
2 tablespoons currant jelly

Place the flour, butter and salt in a food processor. Switching the machine on and off quickly, blend only until the pieces of butter are evenly distributed and coated with flour. Do not overprocess.

With the machine running, again in on-and-off pulsating motions, pour the ice water into the flour mixture through the feed tube. Add only enough water to form a cohesive, but not sticky, mass.

Remove the mixture from the processor and press the pastry together, using the heel of your hand. Gently pat the pastry into a rectangle 8 by 12 inches. Fold into three as you would a business letter. Wrap in plastic and chill for an hour.

Heat the oven to 400 degrees.

Roll the dough on a lightly floured board into an even 10-by-18-inch rectangle. Cut 4 ½-inch strips along the length of the rectangle. Brush the edges with the egg and place the dough strips on top to make a rim all the way around. Trim the strips on the short side.

Place on a baking sheet. Prick the bottom with a fork. Bake in the preheated oven for 15 to 20 minutes, or until done.

Set aside to cool.

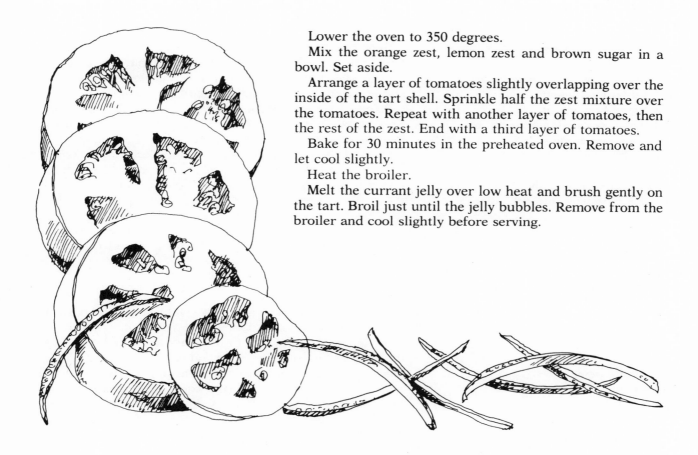

Lower the oven to 350 degrees.

Mix the orange zest, lemon zest and brown sugar in a bowl. Set aside.

Arrange a layer of tomatoes slightly overlapping over the inside of the tart shell. Sprinkle half the zest mixture over the tomatoes. Repeat with another layer of tomatoes, then the rest of the zest. End with a third layer of tomatoes.

Bake for 30 minutes in the preheated oven. Remove and let cool slightly.

Heat the broiler.

Melt the currant jelly over low heat and brush gently on the tart. Broil just until the jelly bubbles. Remove from the broiler and cool slightly before serving.

Pear Shortcake

Serves 12 to 14

This recipe is a festive-looking creation of my own based on components I like for lots of other recipes. Considering the richness of the elements, it is a surprisingly light dessert that will not feel like a surfeit after a large dinner. The cake can be assembled hours in advance, and the components can be prepared days ahead of time. Finished, the cake is a handsome but not gaudy array of colors.

This cake is neither very sweet nor very heavy, so that a wine with a hint of sweetness will be just right. Look for a Johannisberg Riesling with a small amount of residual sugar or, for a glamorous dinner, a bubbling wine.

This cake can be served at lunch after a salad or simple grilled fish, and the same wine can be used throughout the meal. It can also be the summation of an elegant dinner at which a variety of wines is served.

2 9-inch Light Sponge Cakes (see recipe)

⅓ cup apple jelly, heated with 1 tablespoon water

2 cups heavy cream

3 tablespoons confectioners' or superfine sugar

2-3 tablespoons poire (pear-flavored white alcohol)

12 Poached Pear halves (see recipe), cut crosswise into thin slices

Raspberry Sauce (see recipe)

Slice the sponge cakes horizontally into 2 layers each. Brush the top of each layer with some apple-jelly glaze.

Whip the cream until it begins to thicken. Add the sugar and poire and continue to beat until very stiff.

Place 1 layer of cake on a serving platter, glazed side up. Spread with a layer of whipped cream about ¼ inch thick. Reserving the prettiest pear slices for the top, place a quarter of the slices over the cream in an even layer. Repeat with 2 more layers of cake, cream and pears. Top with the last layer of cake, glazed side up. Frost the entire cake with the remaining cream. Overlap the reserved pear slices in a neat circle around the outer edge.

Just before serving, pour Raspberry Sauce over the center of the top and on the platter around the base of the cake.

POACHED PEARS

Makes 12 pear halves

8 cups water

1 cup sugar

2 cloves

3-inch stick cinnamon

1 vanilla bean

1 lemon

6 pears

Place the sugar and water in a 2½-quart saucepan. Bring the water to a boil and add the cloves, cinnamon and vanilla bean. Squeeze the juice of the lemon into the syrup and add the squeezed halves. Peel, core and halve the pears. Add the pear halves, cores and peelings to the pot. The pears should be completely covered with the liquid; if they are not, add more water and sugar (2 tablespoons sugar per cup water).

Simmer the liquid until the pears are soft enough to be pierced through with a skewer. Cooking time will depend on the firmness of the pears. Remove the pears with a slotted spoon and let cool.

RASPBERRY SAUCE

Makes about 2 cups

Raspberries have one of the world's best flavors. Although they are expensive and prone to spoilage, they fortunately seem to suffer less than any of the other berries when frozen. In the summer, I pick raspberries and make a fresh version of this sauce to eat immediately and some to freeze for winter. The overwhelming dividend is the sweet, rich perfume that fills my kitchen.

This sauce is scrumptious with homemade ice cream or poached fruit.

2 10-ounce packages frozen raspberries, packed in syrup, and defrosted

Juice of 1 lemon

Place the berries and lemon juice in a food processor fitted with the steel blade and process until smooth. For a seedless sauce, push the mixture through a fine sieve.

Light Sponge Cake

I am really very pleased with this recipe as it makes high, light, and—at the same time—tender layers. After reading many old cookbooks, I found that the trick was to reduce the gluten content as far as possible while still providing enough gluten so the batter will stretch and rise. I found that this balance of cake flour and cornstarch—no baking powder—seems to do the trick optimally.

While I use this Light Sponge Cake in the preceding Pear Shortcake, it is also good simply dusted with powdered sugar and cut into wedges. To make it more attractive, place a paper doily on the cake and use it as a template to be dusted with a thin layer of sifted powdered sugar. Gingerly remove the doily to preserve the pattern.

7 large eggs, separated and at room temperature
1 cup plus 1 tablespoon sugar
1 tablespoon boiling water
1 teaspoon vanilla extract or
½ teaspoon freshly grated lemon rind
¾ cup cake flour, aerated
¼ cup cornstarch, aerated

Lightly grease and flour 2 9-inch cake pans. Heat the oven to 350 degrees.

Place the egg yolks in a mixing bowl. Using the electric mixer, beat for about 30 seconds, or until the eggs begin to thicken. Gradually beat in 1 cup sugar and continue beating until very thick, about 2 minutes.

Stir in the boiling water and flavoring. Gently fold in the flour and cornstarch, about a third at a time.

In a clean bowl, beat the egg whites with an electric mixer. When frothy, add the remaining tablespoon sugar and beat until soft peaks form. Stir about a quarter of the whites into the cake batter to lighten, then fold in the remaining whites.

Divide the batter evenly between the pans. Place them, not touching, on the middle rack of the oven and bake for 20 to 30 minutes, or until the cake springs back when pushed lightly with your finger. Remove from the oven and cool in the pans on a wire rack for about 10 minutes. Run a spatula or knife around the outer edges of the cakes to loosen, then turn out onto the rack to cool completely.

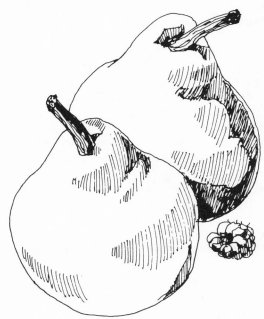

Pineapple-Bourbon Cheesecake

Serves 12 to 14

Good cheesecakes abound. Today we should say "American as cheesecake" rather than "as apple pie." For this recipe, the pineapple is folded into the cheesecake mixture rather than sitting wetly on top. It keeps the cheesecake extra moist and light. The tastes of the bourbon and ginger blend with that of the pineapple until it is hard to tell them apart. The crust is a cookie dough. It is a little difficult to handle, but worth the effort.

FOR THE CRUST:

½ cup sugar
Grated rind of 1 lemon
Grated rind of 1 orange
1 cup all-purpose flour
¼ pound unsalted butter, cut into
    8 pieces
1 egg yolk

FOR THE FILLING:

1 cup bourbon
1 slice fresh ginger, peeled
20-ounce can pineapple chunks,
    drained
5 8-ounce packages cream cheese
1¾ cups sugar
3 tablespoons all-purpose flour
Grated rind of 1 lemon
¼ teaspoon vanilla extract
5 large eggs
2 egg yolks

Begin by making the crust. Heat the oven to 400 degrees.

Place the sugar, rinds and flour in a food processor and process until just mixed. Add the butter and process until the mixture resembles coarse meal. Add the egg yolk and process until the mixture barely comes together.

Wrap the dough in plastic and chill for 1 hour.

Roll out one-third of the dough between 2 sheets of wax paper into a 9-inch circle. Fit it over the bottom of a 9-inch springform pan. Bake in the preheated oven for about 8 minutes, or until brown.

Roll the remaining dough between wax paper into a strip just under 2 inches wide. Fit the dough into the sides of the pan. Fit the sides over the bottom and press the dough over the bottom so it forms a tight seal. Refrigerate until the filling is ready.

To make the filling, start by heating the oven to 550 degrees.

Place the bourbon in a food processor. With the machine running, drop in the ginger to mince. Stop the machine and add the pineapple. Process until shredded.

Place the cream cheese, sugar, flour, rind and vanilla in the bowl of an electric mixer. Beat until very smooth, then beat in the whole eggs, one at a time, followed by the yolks. Then beat in the pineapple mixture until blended.

Pour the batter into the prepared pan. Bake in the preheated oven for 10 minutes, then reduce the heat to 200 degrees and bake 1 hour longer, or until set.

Remove from the oven and cool on a wire rack. When cool, run a knife around the edge and then remove the springform sides.

BASIC RECIPES

In the previous recipes, I call for a lot of stocks and glazes made from stocks. I do this because I like to minimize labor and at the same time have a lot of flavor in my food. Stocks can be made in quantity and don't have to be watched. They yield enormous dividends and will last for months in the freezer. When I am in a hurry or don't have stocks on hand, I either find another recipe or use a canned stock. Canned chicken stock is usually better than canned beef stock, so I generally use it in beef recipes—substituting it entirely for the beef stock, or combining two-thirds chicken with one-third beef stock—to get better flavor.

For a quick glaze, sprinkle ½ package unflavored gelatin over 1 cup cold chicken stock in a stainless steel pot. Let sit for a few minutes until the stock has absorbed all the gelatin, then boil it until it is reduced to about 1½ tablespoons. (If making a larger quantity, use a wide sauté pan for quicker results.)

The one thing I have to be careful about is salt. Canned stocks are generally salty and, if reduced, become saltier still. Nevertheless, by omitting the salt called for in most recipes, you can get away with a salty reduction.

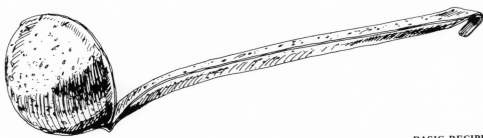

Chicken Stock

5- to 6-pound chicken, or 6 pounds chicken bones, necks and wings

Place the chicken in a stock pot with just enough water to cover. Bring the water to a boil and skim off the fat and scum that rise to the top. Lower the heat so the liquid is just barely boiling and continue cooking for 8 to 12 hours, skimming from time to time. The more often you skim, the clearer your stock will be.

Pour the stock through a sieve and let cool at room temperature, then refrigerate. Remove the fat from the surface and any sediment from the bottom.

Use as is, refrigerate, freeze or reduce for Chicken Glaze.

Turkey Stock

Although you can make a good turkey stock using water, it will be richer and fuller if you start with chicken stock.

Carcass of a roasted 8-pound turkey
Gizzard, heart and neck of the turkey
3 quarts chicken stock (see previous recipe)
2 cups coarsely chopped celery with leaves
2 medium-size onions, quartered
2 tablespoons kosher salt
4 medium-size carrots, peeled and cut into chunks
4 fresh sage leaves or 4 sprigs parsley
Few sprigs thyme

Place the carcass, gizzard, neck, heart and chicken stock in a stock pot and bring to a boil. Skim thoroughly. Lower the heat and simmer for 12 hours or longer, skimming from time to time, as needed. The more often you skim, the clearer your stock will be. Add water as needed to keep the level constant.

Strain the stock, discarding the bones. If using for stock, reduce the liquid to 2½ quarts. Cool to room temperature, then refrigerate. Skim off all the fat from the top and remove the sediment from the bottom.

If using for soup, add the remaining ingredients before you slowly reduce the liquid to 2½ quarts. Strain the mixture through a sieve lined with a damp kitchen towel, pressing on the solids to release all the liquid. Cool and refrigerate or freeze until ready to use.

Meat Stock

6 pounds veal bones (preferably knuckles), cut into small pieces
2 pounds beef shin
About 5 quarts water

Heat the oven to 400 degrees.

Place the bones and beef in a roasting pan and cook for 1 to 2 hours, or until very brown. Turn as needed and make sure they don't burn.

Place the meat and bones in a stock pot. Pour out the fat in the pan and discard. Place the roasting pan over medium heat and pour in some water. With a wooden spoon, scrape the bottom of the pan to loosen any caramelized bits. Pour the liquid into the pot.

Add water just to cover and bring to a boil. Lower the heat to a simmer and cook, at a bare simmer, for 12 hours, making sure to keep the level of water constant. Skim often.

Strain through a sieve lined with a damp kitchen towel. Discard the solids. Cool the stock and thoroughly degrease. The stock should be very gelatinous.

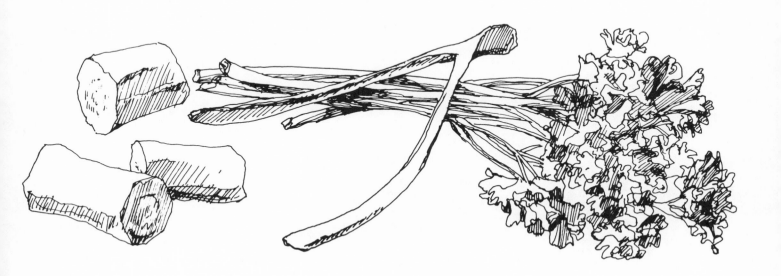

Duck Stock

Duck stock is one of those marvelous bonuses when you are cooking a duck dinner. After your guests have enjoyed all the delicious meat, the remaining bare bones provide a glistening amber broth to enjoy as is or to use in a more complex soup or sauce.

4 duck carcasses, cracked

Place the duck carcasses in a large stock pot and add just enough water to cover the bones. Place over high heat; bring to a boil and remove the scum that rises to the surface.

Reduce the heat so the liquid simmers. Skim the fat and impurities from the surface from time to time. The more often you skim, the clearer your stock will be. Cook for about 12 hours. Discard the solids. Cool the stock, then refrigerate or freeze.

Glazes

All glazes are made in the same way and will keep indefinitely in the freezer.

**1 quart chicken, meat or duck stock
(see previous recipes)**

Pour the stock into a 2-quart saucepan and bring to a boil. Lower the heat and let simmer until the stock is deep brown and syrupy. It may be necessary to transfer the contents to a smaller pot as it reduces. Be careful not to let it burn.

Let cool, then refrigerate or freeze until needed.

Oenological Terms

AGE: *Barrel age.* Time at which, when fermentation is completed, the wine is put to age—mellow and ripen—in a cask, usually made of oak.

Bottle age. The number of years a wine spends in the bottle.

Bottle aging. The continued ripening of the wine in the bottle, made possible by a certain amount of air present in the wine at the moment of bottling.

ALCOHOL BY VOLUME: The percentage of alcohol contained in a wine, the metrically measured strength of that wine. California law dictates that white wines have alcohol contents between 10 and 14 percent and red wines have contents of 10.5 to 14 percent by volume, allowing for a leeway in accuracy of about a degree and a half. The percentage of alcohol must be indicated on the label.

BLENDING: The mixing or marrying of wine from different grapes to make the best whole, or to upgrade an inferior wine with a substantially better wine, to obtain a uniform quality or a product better than any one of its individual components.

FERMENTATION: Process by which the grape sugar, in the presence of naturally occurring and other yeasts, converts into alcohol.

GENERIC: Wine given the name of the specific European wine-growing district from which the grape that produced the wine was originally transplanted (e.g., California Chablis).

PASTEURIZATION: Process of stabilization in which wine is sterilized by quickly heating it while it is still in the barrel. Performed mostly on inexpensive wines, the process destroys all bacteria, thereby rendering the wine unable to change or age.

PROPRIETARY NAME: An individual winery's made-up name for a wine.

ROOT-STOCK: A cutting or entire vine onto which a section of another vine is grafted. The stock provides a healthy, disease-resistant medium for the weaker, tender vine.

SUGAR: *Brix.* Measurement to determine the approximate sugar content of grape juice and sweet wine.

At harvest. The level of sugar at the time of harvest is measured to insure that the amounts of sugar and acid have reached a proper balance to produce the desired wine.

Residual. Any sugar remaining after the yeasts have fermented the grape juice and its natural sugar into wine.

TANNIN: An acid drawn from grape skins, pits and stems and dissolved in the grape juice during fermentation. It is an essential component of red wine, giving it its character and some of its taste, and contributing to its longevity.

VARIETAL: The sole grape of *Vitis vinifera* species used to make a wine, or the dominant such grape in a blended wine, which by California law must be at a level of at least 51 percent. In 1983, this will go up to 75 percent.

VINTAGE: The year the grapes are harvested may be shown on the label. Vintage should not be taken to mean "a very good year." Any wine from a good vineyard will be labeled with the vintage date whether the year was good or poor, though very good vineyards will often forgo producing any wine in a poor year.

VITIS VINIFERA: The vine species from which most of the world's better wine is made. Indigenous to Europe, the species has been transplanted to California and is responsible for a lot of that state's wines. Most notable of other U.S. vine species is *Vitis labrusca*, which grows wild and abundantly in the eastern portion of the country.

Further Reading

PERIODICALS

Robert Finigan's Private Guide to Wines, national and California editions. Robert Finigan, 100 Bush Street, San Francisco, CA 94104; $24 for one year's subscription.

The Friends of Wine. Les Amis du Vin, 2303 Perkins Place, Silver Spring, MD 20910; $15 for one year's subscription.

Vintage Magazine. P.O. Box 2224, New York, NY 10163; $20 for one year's subscription.

BOOKS

Adams, Leon D. *The Wines of America*, 2nd edition, revised. New York: McGraw-Hill Book Co., 1978.

Balzer, Robert Lawrence. *Wines of California.* New York: Harry N. Abrams, 1978.

Chroman, Norman. *The Treasury of American Wines.* New York: Rutledge-Crown Publishers, 1973.

Fadiman, Clifton, and Aaron, Sam. *The Joys of Wine.* New York: Harry N. Abrams, 1975.

Hannum, Hurst, and Blumberg, Robert S. *The Fine Wines of California.* Garden City, NY: Doubleday & Co., Inc., Dolphin Books, 1973.

Olken, Charles, Singer, Earl, and Roby, Norman. *The Connoisseurs' Handbook of California Wines.* New York: Alfred A. Knopf, 1980.

Sunset Books and Sunset Magazine, Editors of (research and text: Bob Thompson). *Guide to California's Wine Country*, 2nd edition. Menlo Park, CA: Lane Publishing Co., 1979.

Thompson, Bob, and Johnson, Hugh. *The California Wine Book.* New York: William Morrow and Co., 1976.

Wine Consultants of California. *Buying Guide to California Wines*, winter 1975 edition (3rd revised edition in press). San Francisco: Wine Consultants of California.